TRAINING
THE
PERFORMANCE
HORSE

TRAINING THE PERFORMANCE HORSE

FROM WESTERN PLEASURE TO REINING

TERRY THOMPSON
AND
JEANNE O'MALLEY

J. B. LIPPINCOTT COMPANY
NEW YORK

All photographs in this book with the exception of Photo 36 by Johnny Johnston were supplied by Jeanne O'Malley.

Photos 9, 10, and 22 originally appeared in *Horse & Rider*.

Designed by Judith Woracek

U.S. Library of Congress Cataloging in Publication Data

Thompson, Terry.
    Training the performance horse.

      1. Horse-shows—Western division and classes.
2. Horse-training.   I. O'Malley, Jeanne, joint author.
II. Title.   III. Title: Performance horse: from
Western pleasure to reining.   IV. Title: Western
pleasure to reining.
SF296.W47T45   636.1'08'88   79-13614
ISBN-0-397-01371-X

---

85 86 87 88 10 9 8 7 6 5 4 3 2

to Bonnie
to Bill

CONTENTS

Acknowledgments

Our professional debts go back a long time before we decided to write a book. At the top of Terry's list of people owed have to come his parents, Laurence and Vonda Thompson, whose support and encouragement helped make him the man and rider he is today. Right beside them are John and Anna Claire Chesebrough, who gave him the advice, the help, and the opportunities he needed to become a successful and respected horse trainer.

By the same token, Jeanne might never have written about horses if her parents, George and Ellen Theodore, hadn't encouraged her to learn a number of ways of working in the horse industry. She is grateful to them for the preparation they gave her and also to Dr. S. W. Sabin, Cooperative Extension Horse Specialist for New York State, for his faith in her and all the "distinct challenges" he sent her way, not the least of these being a clinic with Terry Thompson.

After that initial meeting, we collaborated on several magazine articles, but it was *Horse & Rider* magazine that inspired us to think in terms of more than 2,000 words when Ray Rich assigned us a six-part series on horse training. He not only encouraged us in this project but generously allowed us to reprint several photographs from the series in this manuscript. Don Pitts, Editor of *The Appaloosa News* and Public Relations Officer for The Appaloosa Horse Club, not only helped us obtain permission to reprint the Appaloosa Reining and Western Riding patterns and rules but also was available, along with many other members and officers of the club, with encouragement and advice over many months of work.

Closer to hand were the riders and trainers who shot photographs, modeled for them, and helped us in too many ways to count. We would like to take this opportunity to thank David Moore, Michael Lake, Mark Turner Carmela Gadler, Pam Ertter, Ellen Wells, and Alice Ann Gasiorowski, without whom everything would have been a whole lot harder.

Finally, because they have always been the bottom line, our thanks to Bonnie Thompson and Bill O'Malley, who corrected our grammar, fixed our spelling, put in the punctuation, fed us, laughed with us, and shared the ups and downs of writing a book on horse training. Without them this book might not have been. It sure wouldn't have been as much fun.

INTRODUCTION

This book was written for the amateur stock-seat competitor, not for the beginner. Horse training is for the advanced or intermediate rider who has ridden Western horses trained by professionals and would like to try training his or her own horse for competition. Horse training is not for small children who have shown made horses, no matter how many equitation ribbons they have won. A teenager who has a lot of sense and patience might be able to do it—working under supervision—but there are few youngsters who can hold their temper and not use a whip to relieve frustration when things go wrong, who have the experience to recognize a horse's errors and correct them, and who have the physical strength to control a young horse that gets out of hand.

However, amateurs with intelligence, some basic instruction and experience, and sufficient time and patience will find it is not impossible to train a Western performance horse. They should have the common sense to ask questions, to grasp ideas, and to make those ideas work for them.

As an amateur, you will have an advantage over the professional trainer: Apart from the experience you'll gain

1

and the money you'll save, if you are dedicated you will probably spend more time with the horse than a professional trainer could. Like many professionals, I have a lot of horses in training, and I ride each of them daily for only as long as it takes that horse to learn the day's lesson.* For a horse that's working well, this would be 30 to 60 minutes each day, five or six days a week. But if you are an amateur who is serious about training and can devote a couple of hours every day for five or six days a week, you can bring a horse on every bit as well as I can. You can work with the horse every evening and, when you're finished, you will probably brush him a little longer than I would, pet him, say nice things to him, take extra time with him. All this will have an effect.

A professional trainer usually can't afford the extra time an amateur can give. Like most, I work under a month-by-month contract. This is my livelihood, and assuming a horse has the potential, it's in my interest to produce that horse as efficiently as I can. I know enough not to rush the process, but I also know I have to ride my string of horses five days a week without fail, whether it's cold, raining, or during a telecast of the Super Bowl game. I can't have a horse backslide, because bringing him back to where he should be will mean a lot of extra hours. Amateurs, on the other hand, find it easy to forget the horse for a few days and let the training program lapse—it doesn't cost them anything but their spare time and maybe their disposition. Another contrast: If I have an accident with a horse and am laid up for a while, it's my tough luck but I've still got my job, whereas if amateurs who hold anything but a sedentary job break a leg , they're not only short a trainer, they may be out of a

*Although the first-person "I"—Terry's voice—is used throughout, the writing of this book represents a true collaboration.

job. This is something for you to consider if the horse in question looks as if he's going to be a problem.

Even with the cleverest and most amiable horse, training is a major commitment in time and effort. You *must* work the horse five days a week for at least the first three months, and the daily work will last at least an hour but more like two. You begin by grooming the horse thoroughly and then longeing him. Tacking him up, working him, and putting him away take at least an hour. Without skimping on any of the work and preliminaries, and by spending one and a half to two hours a day, you can green-break a horse in three months, on an average, just as a professional can.

But unless you can stick to the schedule without fail, you risk doing more harm than good. If you work a horse intensively for five days and then turn him out for a week during your final exams or while you go on vacation, you are getting nothing done—and actually doing worse than nothing. During that short week of no training, the horse is forgetting what he has learned. You come back after a week's absence and can't understand why the horse is not following orders. You think the horse is just being stubborn and proceed to whip the tar out of him, which just confuses him more. What you have not realized is that the horse is a creature of habit and that all training is based on this fact. Habits are not formed in one week or two or three. They are formed by going over and over the same lesson and the same cues for month after month until they become second nature to the horse. If you interrupt the training before the habit is completely formed, the horse quickly forgets it.

In the three months you are green-breaking a horse, you are only taking the first step in forming these habits. Three months will not give anyone a finished horse. In fact, there are a lot of instances when three months of hard work won't even produce a green horse. Three months is a ball-park figure. If the horse is sound, if he doesn't incur any injuries, if he is a reasonable horse, the chances are good that he can be started in Western pleasure shows in three months. But an accidentally pricked sole can keep a horse out of training, a frail horse will have to be brought along more slowly until he can physically do the work . . . there are many variables.

In fact, the only thing you can be sure of is that the horse's preliminary training will not take less than three months. When I was starting out as a trainer, a lot of my troubles came from having the horse for too short a time. I didn't have enough confidence and reputation to say that I must have the horse for three months at least. Many times a client would give me only two months and then take the horse home—and usually not ride the horse again until spring. Then I'd hear comments like "The horse wasn't trained very well" or "The horse isn't what I expected him to be." This was the owner's fault, not the trainer's, and it is a very common one.

Now I tell my clients not to bring me a horse if they aren't going to continue to ride him when they get him home. "If you take that horse home and put him up, you are going to be complaining about the money you wasted on the trainer." I can say that now because I'm established. I have no magic wand to send home with each horse I train. Time is the important element as far as horse training is concerned, and my clients had better be prepared to spend time as well as money if they want a good performance horse. The same thing goes for amateur trainers.

Remember too that every time a horse is ridden, that

horse is being trained. There is no such thing as saying, "We'll just take it easy today and not work." Every time a horse comes in contact with a human being, habits are formed or reinforced. A horse is always being trained. The horse may not realize it, the rider may not realize it, but the training goes on just the same.

As an amateur, you must constantly evaluate both the horse and yourself as trainer. At some point—maybe in connection with teaching lead changes or stops or spins—you may have to recognize your limitations and ask for help. Whether for polishing or for teaching, you may have to seek a professional trainer.

There are several things to keep in mind when selecting a trainer. Look at who is doing a lot of business. This alone won't tell who is the best, but it is one indication. See how the trainer is doing in competition, in shows. If I wanted help in teaching my horse lead changes, I would look for someone who competes in Western Riding classes, not for a pleasure-horse trainer or someone who specializes in halter horses. If the horse is going to be entered in Western Riding, I would not send him to an exclusively reining establishment either. A reining lead change is different. It calls for more speed than a Western Riding lead change. On the other hand, a Western Riding lead change is a good foundation for a future reining horse.

Few people appreciate the importance of keeping a horse upright in a lead change. Most people just flop the horse over and kick him. But successful Western riders make an art of lead changes. So do dressage riders. I would look for a trainer who talks in dressage terms or concepts when asked for advice. (Don't be put off by someone who calls it a "lead change" instead of a "flying lead change," though. The ideas, not the vocabulary, are the important things.)

Look for a person who competes and wins at Western Riding. Look for quietness and smoothness in the patterns. Look for non-speed. I don't want to see *pit, pit, pit—kick, kick, kick—spur, spur, spur.* Look for a trainer whose horses show the desirable qualities of smoothness, collection, and effortless balance, whether your questions are about Western Riding or Western Reining.

In choosing a good professional trainer, convenience should not be an important consideration. Even if you have to drive a long way to get your horse to such a trainer, it will be worth it. Taking a horse to the wrong trainer can mess up the horse, the investment, and all the time you have put into him. So begin with the idea of doing your very best with this horse and give him all the time he needs. If you reach a point where you need a little help, take time here too. Don't quickly snap at the first convenient stable, but consider all of them to find a talented, reputable trainer in whose care the horse will be safe while learning.

CHOOSING A PROSPECT

When I am looking for a prospective performance horse, there is nothing I like better than the mature horse that already gives his head, takes his leads, and is well-balanced. I can evaluate this horse with all the necessary information right in front of me: bloodlines, conformation, temperament, way of going, and the basic training either I or someone I trust has already given him.

When looking at a young horse, though, I have to guess how he is going to look and perform in the future. So if I have a choice, why should I or anyone else be interested in a two-year-old? One reason is that I won't have as much control over the development of a mature horse as I will over that of a young one. With a youngster I won't have to overcome any bad habits or resistances someone else may have put into him. An untrained horse won't have to unlearn anything before his serious schooling starts.

When you're looking for a horse to buy, price is of course a consideration, and in Western horses it is an important one. When you're talking about only a moderately good Appaloosa today, you may be talking $2,500, and that will be considered a bargain. (Once in a while a buyer does stumble onto a good less-expensive horse,

7

but this is like winning the lottery, and it happens just about as often.) If you can get a super horse for $7,500, you've got a steal. If this price is on a two-year-old, it will be a nice-looking halter horse with performance ability. If it is a flashy, nice-looking halter horse with a year of riding behind him, the price can easily go into five figures.

Prices vary from breed to breed. For instance, you can often buy a good Quarter Horse cheaper than a good Paint, Appaloosa, Pinto or Palomino. For one thing, there are more Quarter Horses to choose from and so, by the odds, there are more good ones around. For another, markings or color aren't as important in the Quarter Horse breed as they are in the Paint, Pinto, Appaloosa, and Palomino, where a brightly colored or marked stallion or mare will bring two or three times the price of an equally talented but plainer horse. The color requirements for registration also cut down the number of horses available in those breeds (if you are interested in buying a registered horse).

Being a trainer, I don't always get to choose my horses. I am often stuck with what I've got or with what people send me, and a lot of people who read this book will also have to make do with what they have. However, if I'm in a position to go out and buy a horse, I like to start with a two-year-old. I don't buy a two-year-old thinking that I'm going to show him in performance classes at that age. Instead, I buy him to bring along, to train for the future. When I buy him I don't think of him as *being* a performance horse, I think of training him with an eye to his *becoming* a performance horse.

Before I even see this colt, his bloodlines might give me an idea of how he is going to perform. In every breed there are bloodlines which produce more performance horses than others. In the Appaloosa breed, for instance, the Absarokee Sunset horses are famous lead changers. They are hot and aggressive, but if they're started correctly they always give a balanced, coordinated lead change in front and behind. The Rustler Charger and Little Navajo Joe horses have an aptitude for the sliding stop. Every breed has lines like these. If you are interested in performance horses, you'll be aware of bloodlines and take them into consideration. They aren't an infallible indication, but they will give you an idea of where to start looking.

Your first look at the horse will probably find him on the end of a lead line. Take your time and study his conformation. Personally, I like a medium-coupled horse. I wouldn't ordinarily choose a short-coupled horse, and I sure don't like one with a long back. A long back is often a weak back, and though a short-backed horse is okay, a lot of short-backed horses have short, inflexible necks, which can be a problem. I'm looking for a medium, middle-of-the-road back. I like a slanted croup, dropping down into the horse's hip where it ties down deep into his gaskin. I want it to go down well into the stifle and on into the gaskin. This will help him keep his weight and power underneath him. I also like to see a well-defined set of withers. I don't want them too prominent, but they should hold the saddle on the horse, keep it from slipping off.

The hind legs are a major consideration in a performance horse. I like to see a little sickle in the hocks attached to those big gaskins. A horse that is just a little sickle-hocked, a little camped-under, will find it easier to keep his weight on his hindquarters and to keep those hindquarters under him for more agility. A well-developed gaskin—well-muscled inside as well as outside—helps a horse hold his legs in place and slide straight during the stop.

Some people confuse sickle hocks with cow hocks. Cow hocks are the equivalent of a knock-kneed person *(photo 1)*. They are set very close together, resulting in the feet being far apart or base-wide. Sickle hocks, seen from the side, are set in front of a plumb line dropped through the point of the hip. Cow hocks are the worst thing you can find in a prospective performance horse, especially if you intend to rein him. Not only are they weak in themselves, but when the rider asks for a sliding stop they encourage the horse to spread his legs instead of keeping them under his body for balance. This spreading causes the horse to wallow and slip as his hind legs drift farther and farther apart.

At the front end of the horse, I want to see a nice V and a well-muscled forearm. Once again, I am looking for moderation. A very heavy V and a massive forearm will not help a performance horse. Without being scrawny or underdeveloped, the horse should be light in front while still having a good V. For maximum mobility, I don't want the horse's neck to tie in deep to his chest. Horses like that are luggers. When you pick them up to move, they bounce on their front feet. They never walk out athletically because it's hard for them to move all that bulk smoothly.

Finally, I like a horse with a nice thin neck. A horse with a light neck and a clean throatlatch is more flexible in his neck. A thick-necked horse is not as athletic, and if he gets an idea to do it, he can set that heavy neck and use it against his rider. Sometimes when I find a flexible neck it is upside down, a ewe neck. It is almost physically

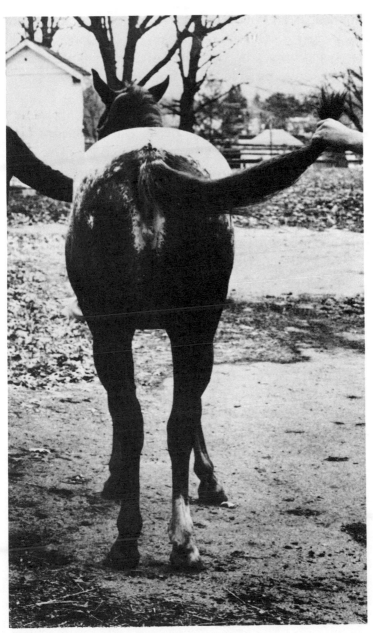

1

impossible for this horse to learn to carry his head properly. He will always be looking at the clouds, he will be going with a hollow back, and, as a performance horse, he will be a dud. The conformation of the horse shown in *photo 2* pleases me in every respect.

The last consideration is probably the most important: how the horse moves. Bloodlines can sometimes fool you, conformation can sometimes fool you; athletic ability, movement, way of going—this is the acid test. I won't buy a horse unless I can see him move. When the horse is trotted in hand, on a lead line, you can check for technical faults in his way of going—like paddling, overreaching, and clipping. But watching him in the pasture or paddock will tell you a lot more. A horse should pick up his feet when he moves, not shuffle along the ground. I want to see a horse clip along, moving his feet about grass height in front so he can remain catlike. A horse that is stiff in front will poke his feet in the ground when he stops and have a tendency to come up in the air. When he is cantering I like to see the hindquarters engaged and automatically changing leads when the horse changes direction. If he doesn't change when running free, I won't buy him. He will always get the rider into trouble. If a horse cannot balance himself alone, he will rarely be able to do it well with a rider on his back. When he stops I like to see the horse stand upright. I like to see a horse try to use himself when he needs to stop. It will be easier to teach this kind of horse to do a sliding stop than the horse that grinds to a halt or trips over his feet in the pasture.

If the horse has been mounted before, and maybe ridden a little in a bosal, this will help me evaluate him because I can then ride him myself as well as watch someone else handle him. If the owner hasn't used spurs

2

on him or jerked him in the mouth, this is a point in a young horse's favor. I'll ask the rider to trot the horse up and down and then push him off into a canter. It's useful at this point to ask for a lead change and see if the horse automatically takes up the correct lead without previous training in doing so.

This tendency to change leads, to try to balance himself correctly, is something I always look for in a young horse. It is an important point with me because I like horses that are naturals, and so should you. When a horse is asked to change leads, it shouldn't go against his natural impulses to give that change. If you buy a horse that already balances himself, it is going to be one less thing to have to teach him, and that will be helpful for both the professional and the amateur.

Admittedly, these are a lot of points to keep in mind when looking at a horse. Even being able to identify these good and bad points takes much study and practice. Giving them the right emphasis in making your decision takes a lot more. If you aren't perfectly confident in your ability to judge a prospective performance horse, ask the advice of a reputable professional horseman or horsewoman. Tell him or her what you are going to do with this horse, what kind of horse you want to make of him. Get a knowledgeable person to help you, and pay for the advice so there will be no doubt in your mind about any shenanigans. Chances are that intermediate riders will get along much better with some expert help than if they try to choose a horse themselves. They may know a lot about riding, but there are so many factors in choosing a horse for advanced work that it is usually better to rely on professional expertise in the final analysis.

Another expert you are going to want to call on is your veterinarian. The vet will x-ray the horse's legs before you agree to buy him, in addition to examining the horse thoroughly. Beauty may be only skin deep, but athletic ability is not, when you are dealing with performance horses. Using all the resources available is only sensible if you are going to put a lot of money and time into the horse you choose.

FOR
WESTERN
PLEASURE:
GREEN-BREAKING

1. BOSAL TRAINING

A trainer does not just get up one morning and decide that this is the day to bit a horse. Like spins, sliding stops, and every other phase of the horse's training, bitting and head carriage need preparation and groundwork.

As an amateur, the chief advantage you have over a professional trainer is the amount of time you can spend on the horse. A professional must produce results faster because a professional is being paid, and being paid by the month. I don't care how strongly clients urge me, "Take your time, take all the time you need." When they come at the end of the month, they want to see their horse being ridden. They do not want to see him being line-driven or longed. They don't care what kind of equipment the horse is wearing. They want to see him ridden around the ring acting like he knows where he is going. But since you're an amateur, you can take your time, use your head, and enjoy the training of your horse.

The first step in this training is to longe the horse quite hard for three or four days (photo 3). It's possible, and in fact preferable, to do this twice a day for short periods rather than for one long session once a day. You can longe the colt once in the morning and again in the afternoon or evening. Practice halting him on the command of "Whoa" while he is being led in hand and then when he is being longed. *Always* remember to put splint boots on your horse when longeing him, even if it is only for a few minutes. Boots are expensive and everyone is tempted to skip them, but they protect a horse's legs from injury and strain, and it's foolish to take a needless chance by forgetting to put them on.

After those few days of nothing but longeing, saddle the horse and longe him a little more, first at the walk and then at the trot. Let the stirrups flop and let the horse get used to them. This may take five minutes or several days, but when the horse is taking the saddle for granted, try leaning across the horse's back or putting a foot in the stirrup for a few seconds while you put weight in it *(photo 4)*.

At this point it becomes very hard to give advice without knowing you or your horse. I don't think the average amateur intermediate rider should put a bit in the horse's mouth at this time, and I personally favor the use of a bosal, or hackamore, instead *(photo 5)*. But so many people misuse a bosal that I don't like to recommend one unless I'm sure the trainer knows how to use one tactfully. This isn't a problem for everyone, but if you are unsure of the delicacy of your hands, wrap the underside of the bosal with sheepskin or acrylic wool. It won't have a lot of feel, and the horse might go bye-bye sometime, but this is the only way I know to prevent accidental damage to the horse's mouth and nose.

To introduce the horse to the bosal, first longe him thoroughly with his saddle on. Put on the bosal and tie the reins very loosely and lightly to the cinch in a quick-release knot. Tie one rein slightly shorter than the other, and then take the horse into a box stall. If a box stall is

3

4

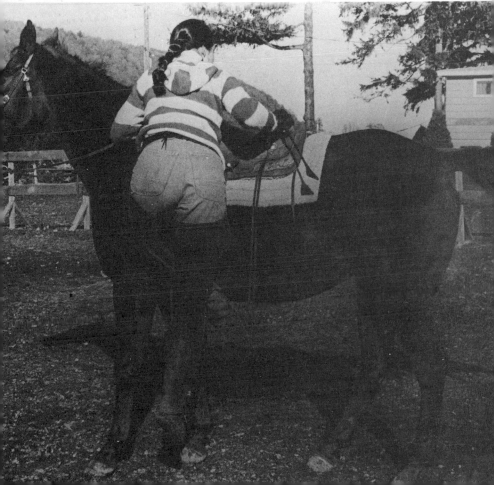

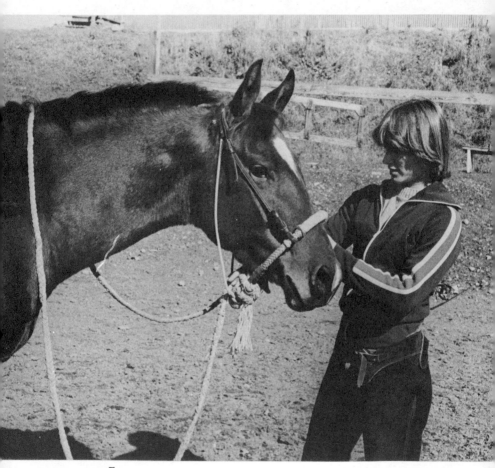

5

unavailable, a very small paddock or riding ring can be used. Just make sure it is sturdy, completely empty of horses and equipment such as jumps, and has nothing like protruding hooks for the horse to get caught on.

Leave him in the stall or small ring for 10 or 15 minutes. Then loosen the short side and tie him the other way. If you're pressed for time, you can tie the horse to the right for those first few minutes one evening and to the left the next night.

What you've done is devise a bitting rig using the bosal and saddle to teach the horse to give his head to pressure on either side. If you have an actual commercial bitting rig, this can be used if you substitute the bosal for the bridle. However, using a saddle does have the advantage of gradually building up your horse's back, getting it accustomed to carrying weight. Also, many young horses react violently to a crupper under the tail. But whichever rig you use, it is important to remember always to longe the horse first and to resist the temptation to tie the horse around too tightly. A lot of people want to snub their horse's nose to his elbow the first day, but even at the height of his training and flexibility the horse won't be tied any tighter than a 40-degree angle.

The first few times, ask for only a few degrees of bend, or flexion. One object of this lesson is to make the horse more supple, not to shred his muscles, and therefore we don't want to make this rig into a solid device. It works on the principle that when the horse moves out of the bend he gets a tap or pressure on the nose that ceases the second he gives his nose to the bend. Thus the horse is rewarded instantly, something very few trainers can produce with their hands. The horse doesn't associate the discipline or taps with the trainer but is teaching himself.

As he learns to give to the pressure of the bosal in either direction, he becomes that much more controllable, and his mouth has not been risked in the process.

When the horse is bending to the right and left, it is time to get on him. Here a lot of people disagree with me, preferring to line-drive a horse before riding him. I might drive a truly rank horse, but when you drive a horse, the first thing you must do is stick a bit in his mouth. The driver is pulling that mouth, bruising it, and maybe getting the horse to overflex, which aggravates and frightens him. I don't want to risk this. This is why I am not a big advocate of line-driving at this point.

After I get some of the horse's confidence, I can shake that confidence once in a while, but I don't want to tear it up first thing by going for the soft tissues of the mouth in order to gain control of him. I cannot agree with putting a bit in a young horse's mouth before he has gained a little confidence and balance.

Instead of line-driving, I would ask a friend, a good-hearted soul, to come over for the afternoon. I would put a bosal on my horse and a halter over that. I wouldn't use a tie-down because if the horse does rear up he will hit the tie-down, and this will just compound his fear.

I would mount the horse quietly, taking the reins in both hands. He won't be afraid, because I've tried my weight in the stirrup before this and put weight on his back. My friend will lead the horse around the arena on a longe line attached to the halter, while I sit quietly in the saddle, not using my legs for cues (photo 6). I would practice saying "Whoa" at the same time I put pressure on the reins and the leadsman puts pressure on the longe line. Pretty soon the horse will get the idea.

After a few minutes of this, my friend can lengthen the

longe line and ask the horse to walk around in a big circle
(photo 7). It may be hard for the horse to balance both
my weight and his own, so I won't be surprised if he walks
unevenly or slowly. I won't use my legs on him to create
more speed. At this point he wouldn't know what the
signal meant. Only when the horse begins to relax will I
start squeezing with my legs at the same time the
leadsman says "Get up" or snaps his whip. I will walk and
trot, and I won't worry if the horse breaks into a canter, as
long as he is balanced on the longe line. But I will make
sure that the circle he is working is the biggest possible,
right out on the end of the line, because it's easier for a
horse to keep his balance on a big circle than on a small
one. It won't surprise me if he moves out pretty fast at
first—most horses do when they are learning to balance
themselves.

No matter what happens, I'll leave control of speed and
direction to the person longeing, and only gradually will I
introduce the bosal reins as a way of bending the horse
around the curve.

Naturally, this progression from walk to trot to canter is
spaced over many days. Again, I'm careful to put splint
boots on the horse's legs every time he is longed. If he is
particularly unbalanced and unsteady I'll use bell boots
too, the kind that jumping horses use to protect their
coronet bands while jumping or galloping cross country.

Each day after I've longed the horse and worked him in
his bosal, I'll tie him around in his stall or a small arena
just as I did at first. When a rider pulls on a bosal, he pulls
on it directly from the bottom, but the side of the bosal
generally comes into play and pokes the horse some-
place. Another drawback is that when working a young
horse in a bosal, especially one wrapped in sheepskin,

6

7

you haven't got a lot of control over him. The horse can start putting his nose up in the air out of the line of control, and thus he is able to run through a bosal if he gets the inclination.

So when I feel I can steer the horse with the bosal reins alone, and don't have to depend on the longe line at all, I will probably introduce a tie-down, *if he needs it.* Once the tie-down is fitted loosely—just tight enough to keep the horse's head from rising beyond the point of control—I longe the horse in this new piece of equipment. If he is going to resist it, he will do it right away, and I can handle this best from the ground.

Sometimes I have a horse that naturally carries his head in a working position, or one that has no head resistances, and then of course I don't need to use a tie-down. With an Arabian or similar horse, which often seems to go naturally in a balanced frame, I will also skip using a tie-down. But with a cold-blooded horse that resists by putting his head in the air, a tie-down is very effective. In any case, if I needed it I would use a tie-down and bosal combination for two or three days only, and then I'd go on to the next step.

This step is what I call an iron bosal, though it can be made from a variety of metals. This piece of equipment is available in tack shops, or it can be ordered by mail. An alternative is a simple stud ring or breeding ring, but I prefer an iron bosal. When using a stud ring, the rider is muscling the horse's whole head from a solid, fixed device, whereas with an iron bosal the rider is allowed more precision. I can flex my fingers and get a little give. Other advantages are that I don't have to tear up the horse's chin (which is a possibility with a regular bosal), and I don't tear up his nose. If I really need to be firm with a horse, the most I will have to do is take off a little hair from the bridge of his nose where he can spare it. I can keep out of his mouth and off his chin, which is important to me.

The iron bosal is used exactly like the sheepskin-covered one and is fitted the same way. It can be used with a tie-down when and if necessary *(photo 8)*. Again, the horse's head should be tied around a few degrees each way for a few minutes daily in the stall or ring. It has the same advantages as a regular bosal: I can take hold of a horse without using brute force, it keeps his head in a controllable position, and it protects his tender mouth and chin. Although it looks severe, an iron bosal can be used successfully on hot-blooded horses like Arabians and Thoroughbreds. I've found they work very well in it and go quite calmly.

The only limitation of an iron bosal is that it isn't an effective deterrent to the chronic runaway. But then, I don't buy that kind of horse and I won't accept it for training. If you have bought a horse like that, thinking he is high-couraged, I'd advise you to get rid of the animal. Buying a habitual runaway is a big mistake. No one needs this kind of horse. A runaway is not the same as a spirited horse, though. If the horse is just a little hot, I longe him well and turn him out often to let him get rid of his energy before I ask him to work. So many people mess up this kind of horse by taking him out of his stall and jumping on immediately to fight him daily. After being belted and hauled into submission, that horse is not going to cooperate with confidence.

Why fight him when it's unnecessary? Longe the horse and let him get rid of his playfulness. Get him ready to pay attention. Maybe it's a bore for the trainer to stand in

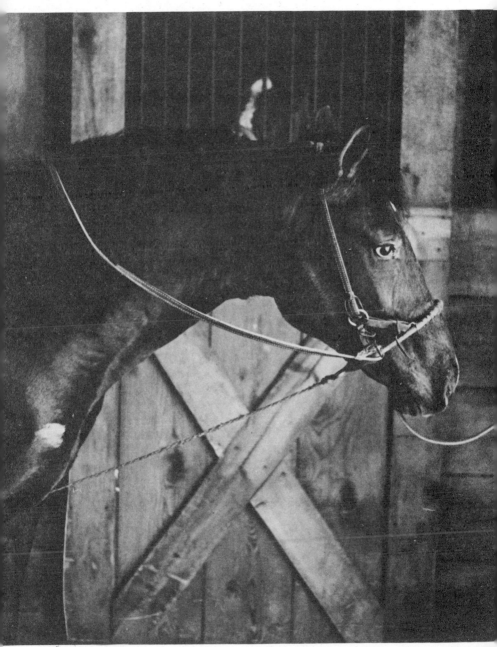

the middle of the arena watching the horse go around, but longeing is such a good training aid. Trot the horse, let him kick off into a canter. Give your horse time to settle down, and each lesson is off to a good start.

Then get on and ride him in big circles in his iron bosal. Walk and trot the horse, but don't ask for the canter for a long time, because it takes him longer to get his balance at that gait. When he can walk and trot and turn in the iron bosal easily and lightly, then and only then do I begin working on his canter.

2. CANTERING

I believe that a young horse can be green-broke in the middle of his second year. This is not too early to canter a young, physically fit horse, but it is too early to ask him to canter slowly, especially for long distances. In too many cases, however, as soon as the young horse learns some basic commands and signals, his owners want to throw him into Western Pleasure competition. Unfortunately, success in these classes seems to be based on how slowly a young horse can canter. What encourages owners to make this mistake are the two-year-old pleasure-horse futurities and the terrific prestige and money to be won in them. These classes, or at least the way they are judged now, are the equivalent of two-year-old racing, but instead of asking a young horse to go too fast, these classes force him to go too slow. The risks are the same. If either the racing or the pleasure colt manages to survive this introduction to his life's work without major leg problems, it is a minor miracle.

In their haste to get into pleasure futurities, too many riders forget to put the horse through basic training. They bit their horse the first day and ride him until he is too tired to resist any more. By their second horse show these young horses hate Pleasure class and hate being ridden. I can't afford to take a chance on that kind of an attitude, or on the leg injuries that are so common. My horses have to learn a lot more than Western Pleasure, and because their work is so challenging they have to like it. It is very difficult for a horse to learn to canter under the weight of a rider, and a pleasure-horse canter is quite collected. One colt in two hundred is ready to produce this kind of collection so early in his training.

Cantering is fun and exciting, and it's usually more comfortable than trotting, so there is a great temptation to skip over the trotting and the work with the bosal and get right into running around in circles. The trouble with skipping the work in the bosal and the tying around is that the trainer is skipping the basis of the horse's head set.

A head set—how the horse carries his head and neck—can be pretty, but, more important, it is an indication of how the horse is carrying himself and how he is balanced. The work with the bosal is teaching him to yield to pressure and to carry his head at about a 45-degree angle. At the same time, the rider is using his legs to keep the horse's rear end underneath him. When the head comes in and the hind legs come under, then the horse has a true head set, true balance. Many times trainers just tie the horse's head the way they want it and ignore the rest of him. The horse has a terrific head carriage, but his rear end will be dragging behind, he will be going with a hollow (and therefore weak) back, and he will not be able to balance his rider's weight with maximum comfort and ease. When this rider demands the slow canter on top of this unbalanced posture, the horse will be cantering in front and trotting behind because he is off-balance. This is the four-beat canter everyone complains about.

It is true that some horses, in spite of the best training in the world, are natural four-beat canterers. They are born doing it just like Tennessee Walking Horse colts run-walk and pacers pace. If the colt in question has a four-beat canter, then he is not going to shine as a Western Pleasure horse. With this horse, the trainer would want to take special pains with his head set and pay a lot of attention to his balance. Faulty balance is the most common cause of a four-beat canter, and this problem can often be solved by letting the horse canter on, letting him free up and go a little faster, a little more extended than the slow pace demanded of him.

To begin any young horse in cantering, I warm him up by trotting him in big circles in the arena or ring. Any dressage rider will tell you that trotting is a horse's learning gait. It's easy for him to balance himself and his rider because the trot is a two-beat diagonal gait. Trotting relaxes him. I trot my young horse in both directions on the circle until he feels relaxed and at ease.

When I ask for the canter, I want to help the horse hold his balance, so I keep my reins in both hands and bridge them across his neck (photo 9). I keep a constant contact on the horse with my legs and hands (through the reins), because the horse isn't ready yet to take full responsibility for holding himself upright and in balance. Just as a beginning ice skater needs all possible support, so a young horse needs firm contact when he begins to canter with a rider.

Some horses just naturally take the correct lead, but others need a little help, and this is where the iron bosal comes in handy. Because he bends easily now, I turn the horse's head slightly to the rail. I squeeze with my outside leg and lift him into the canter. At first I will let the horse go into the canter any way he wants to. Most of them trot a few strides before they take up the canter, because they aren't sure what the trainer wants. But that doesn't bother me. In the beginning all I want is the correct motion. If the horse wants to go on his forehand a little, okay. If he takes the wrong lead, okay. I'll let him canter a little on the wrong lead, and then I'll bring him gently down to the trot and ask again.

The reason so many people run into trouble when asking their young horses to canter for the first time is that they try to help the horse by leaning forward and giving him all the rein he wants *(photo 10)*. Hunt-seat riders call this "throwing the reins at him," and that's pretty much the case. This is just like teaching people to ride a bicycle by putting them on, giving the bike a healthy shove, and then stepping back to watch what happens. A young horse needs support and "trainer wheels" when he is learning to canter. My hands and legs are his trainer wheels, and I don't want to throw them away. A steady hand is a hard thing for an amateur to maintain at the canter, especially if you are used to working with the loose reins demanded in showing. No matter how odd it feels, don't release the horse until you feel him pick up the lead. Then release him slightly, but don't drop the rein contact altogether.

Later, as the young horse learns side-passing, you will be able to dispense with the idea of turning the horse's head slightly to the outside for the canter. As he learns to yield to the pressure of the rider's leg, the horse's sides will become more sensitive, and his cue for the canter will be a step of side pass to the rail. But now, to give him the idea of putting his weight on his inside hind leg, I turn his head slightly away from the lead. *Slightly* is the key word

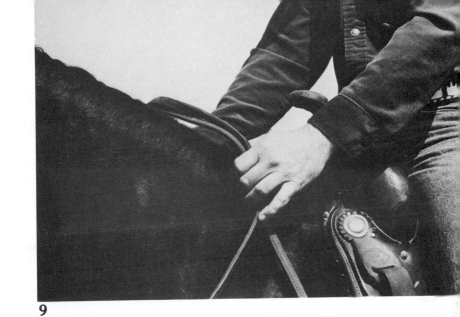

9

10

11

here. So many riders snap the horse's head around to their outside knee so the horse is off-balance, twisted into an incorrect bend and unable to see where he is going. To avoid this mistake, consider that the horse's head is turned to the outside when you can see his outside (rail-side) eyeball or, better still, his outside eyelash.

Instead of following the natural impulse to lean forward, shift your weight onto your outside hip and sit straight *(photo 11)*. It will feel as if you are leaning backward and interfering with your horse no end, but the truth is that you will be in balance and making the horse's job that much easier.

When I start a horse I will canter him four or five times around the arena. If he can canter around a big circle four times without breaking into a trot, that's wonderful. But this is just a goal. It should be approached slowly. At first be satisfied with short canters of once around or even halfway around the arena. Let the horse find his rhythm and balance. It will take him some time and it cannot be rushed. Taking a young horse out to an empty field and cantering him until he is ready to drop is a crash course in cantering—in every sense of the word.

3. BITTING

Nothing influences a horse's future like his bitting. Whether his specialty will be reining, pleasure, gymkhana, or whatever, how he packs his bridle *is* the length and success of a horse's career. Bitting and the carriage it produces are a horse's alphabet, his basics. How he learns to go on the bit is the difference between a career soured after one season and many years of useful work.

There are many ways to start a horse properly in his bridle, and they all have different things going for them. The methods I use are easy and practical. They differ from most methods in that they use a lot of control to teach the horse the proper head position quickly rather than letting him figure it out alone by trial and error. It works on the principle that when the horse is beginning his training he needs a good deal of help from his equipment and rider, and then, as he gets more experience, he can take the responsibility for his position and balance and therefore needs less bit and less contact.

So far, the horse has learned three of his five basic skills in his bosal: side pull (or bend to pressure) from the left, side pull from the right, and flex. The flexing has come from halting the horse in his bosal. He feels the pressure on his nose and halts, yielding his jaw. He has learned

38

these three basic motions, and he has learned how to perform them under the weight of a rider while still retaining his sensitive mouth. Later he will learn two more basic skills: side pass to the left and side pass to the right.

Now, however, he is ready to learn to yield to the bit's pressure just as he did to that of the bosal. His tie-down has started his head set. It kept him from lifting his head past the point of control and has brought his nose in when necessary. Now it is time to refine this position, so that the horse packs his bridle and rider even more easily.

But not too easily. I want my horse to stay in his bridle comfortably, but not so comfortably that he ignores it. That's why I don't clip a rubber bit to his halter for him to wear in the stall. If I did, the horse would eat and drink with his bit on. He would gnaw it and play with it, and soon he would be ignoring it completely.

Instead, I bridle the horse with a mild snaffle bit and then add a rawhide noseband, which holds the mouth closed on the bit. I remove the reins from the bridle and leave the horse alone in the stall to get used to this new equipment. The noseband, or "mouthpiece," is very important. I never ride without one when training, because it prevents the horse from opening his mouth or crossing his jaw. A dressage rider might use a dropped noseband to solve this problem, but I prefer to avoid contact with the chin groove at this time. With an open mouth or crossed jaw, a horse can evade the action of the bit, and it is easier to keep him from learning this trick than it is to break him of the habit once he has learned it.

After the horse has worn the bridle in his stall for a few minutes, I'll put the bosal on over the bridle and warm him up in it. The bosal is controlling the horse, and he is just getting used to the bit by carrying it in his mouth. The next day or so, I'll take off the bosal and ride my horse in a gag snaffle. Why a gag over a regular Western snaffle? For one thing, it doesn't have a chain or strap under the chin, so it doesn't hurt the horse there if he tosses his head. For another, it is a nice soft bit to start a horse on. Most horses get along well with it. There's nothing complicated or mysterious about it, no secrets of the trade. I just find it has more give, more flexibility, than a set bit, and I can lift the horse's head if I have to.

My gag bits don't have leather crownpieces. They have cables that go behind the horse's ears. A lot of people use rope here, but I prefer cable because it has more delicacy and more precision to work on the nerves that run over between the ears. It also does not wear the horse's hair off. By playing on these nerves, I have more control over the horse's head position. My horse starts his progress toward going on the bit without realizing it. Many people ignore this area of the horse, but people who use a double bridle discovered it a long time ago. It has many advantages. It is sensitive enough to be receptive to signals, and it is a nice alternative to going to the horse's mouth to teach him to lower his head. I am a fanatic about staying out of a horse's mouth as much as I can. If I can teach a horse something by pushing on his nose or poll instead of the soft tissues of his mouth, I will.

For the first few days of using this bridle, I don't ask anything of my horse. I just ride him around the ring or arena in his gag snaffle and mouthpiece and let him get used to them. I will bit him in his stall, but always with a bosal over the bit. I never tie him around in the bit. He already knows how to bend, and besides there is the danger that he might rear up and hit against the bit. A gag won't cut his tongue and scare him to death, but I want to spend a lot of time riding him before I actually start tying him around in his stall.

So for several days I ride him in circles at the walk and trot, and maybe try a canter. I keep the reins in both hands and hold them lightly *(photo 12)*. After working him, I'll take him into his stall and tie the reins very lightly and loosely to the cinch for a few minutes *(photo 13)* but I don't leave him in the stall alone like this. Such riding and tying goes on for a full month. The horse senses the similarity between the bit and the bosal and adjusts to this new equipment easily, as long as I don't rush him.

I ride the horse in the gag bit for two or three weeks. As his balance improves, he can take more responsibility for his position, and I can put him in an Argentine or Tom Thumb snaffle. Either is good, but I like the Argentine because it has a copper mouthpiece, which encourages a horse to salivate and relax his jaw. Horses generally seem to get along with them a little better than with other bits.

If the horse carries his head too high, I'll ride him in his Argentine snaffle with a running martingale snapped to the breastplate. The downward pressure holds his head where I want it—in a working position and not up in my face. I won't use a martingale with a horse that doesn't need it, only with those that do, as a deterrent. A running martingale doesn't act unless it's needed. It is not a punishment in itself. It is just like a whip—it can be carried all day and the horse won't even know it's there, until it is needed.

Another piece of equipment I can use to teach a horse how to carry himself is a set of draw reins, or "ropes." In order to use these effectively, you must have very light, sensitive hands. One jerk and the horse can go over backward. It is something that requires a lot of judgment

12

13

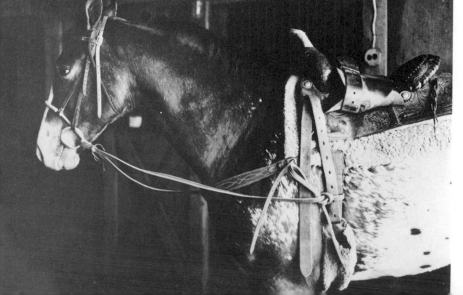

and finesse on your part, but if you have it, the horse will understand quickly and painlessly what is wanted.

If you have trouble, just bit the horse in his stall or ring and leave him there for half an hour. Come back and ride him again. If he gives to the bit, even a little, praise him and get right off. Quitting work is his reward. Don't fight the horse if he is having a bad day. Instead, bit him in his stall and let him think about it. Chances are the horse will soon get bored and start to think, *I'd better start paying attention or I'm going to be in this stall forever.*

4. BACKING

When I judge horses, backing is important to me, regardless of the class. I like to see a horse back nicely, and I wouldn't ask an entry to back if I wasn't going to count it in my placings, and count it a lot. You'd better believe that old Terry is going to knock you dead if you walk into the lineup to perform a back and the horse throws his head in the air or opens his mouth. On the other hand, some judges ask for a back only as a matter of form and don't pay attention to how it is performed. I often wonder why they even bother to ask for this test if they aren't going to evaluate it.

But if judges differ on how much emphasis to put on backing, they do agree on what makes a good backup: The horse flexes at the poll, yields his jaw, keeps his mouth closed, and walks backward in a straight line, his legs moving in diagonal pairs *(photo 14).*

There is no difference in form or speed between a back in a Western Pleasure class, in a Western Reining class, or in a Western Riding class. Speed has nothing to do with correct backing. Accuracy and balance and smoothness do. If I call for a back of three steps in a Pleasure class, that's what I want to see. If the reining pattern calls for a back to the pylon in a Reining class, the pylon is where

44

you stop. If you back any farther, you not only lose out on getting any extra points, you also show that you're a little inaccurate and haven't done the pattern correctly. I see a lot of riders run their horses backward, and many riders get carried away doing it. They hear the crowd and the wind in their ears, and before they know it they've backed out of the arena and out of the class.

Learning this smooth, accurate back can be pretty confusing for a young horse. For one thing, he can't see where he is going, and that's going to make him reluctant to go backwards. For another, it is the first time his rider has really taken up a firm contact on his mouth and has asked for something through the mouth. This is where tact becomes important.

If you take hold of the reins and try to haul the horse back by force, you will probably get the horse's head in your face. The horse has no idea what he's being asked to do, and he'll just keep lifting his head higher and higher as you keep pulling harder and harder.

This doesn't need to happen. If the horse has been started correctly and has been bitted in his stall, he is already familiar with the idea of moving his head away from pressure. You may want to start teaching him to back in a bosal. You may have backed him in a halter to line him up square in Halter classes. It is possible, and a lot of trainers do it, just as many trainers don't want to teach a horse to back until he is completely balanced and comfortable in his bit, because they feel it gives the horse the idea of going behind the bit. (Going behind the bit is when the horse tucks his chin to his chest and evades the bit's action.) But whether or not this is the horse's first experience with backing, it will be his first experience of backing by being asked through his mouth.

Your horse has learned to give to either side and to yield his jaw, and he will give way to yielding his body. Generally he will back the first time you ask correctly. By *correctly* I mean in a manner that is going to eliminate confusion and panic.

To do this, take your reins in both hands. Sit up straight. Don't look at your hands or your saddle horn, because if you do, you won't be able to see if the horse is backing straight and you won't be able to correct his position. Also, by leaning forward you throw your weight onto your horse's front end and make it more difficult for him to move. Instead, put your calves on the horse's sides to alert him. Hold one rein on contact while "asking" with the other. To ask, close your fingers on the rein, taking up a stronger contact, like squeezing out a sponge. Do not lift your asking hand, since this raises the horse's head and hurts his mouth. As soon as you feel the horse take a tentative step back, release the pressure on the asking rein. Then ask with the other rein. When you are asking and releasing in time with the horse's steps, you will be producing a smooth backup. At that time you can go to asking with one hand as in competition.

There are two important things to keep in mind when teaching your horse to back. One is to release the rein instantly when the horse takes even the smallest step backward. That release is his reward. The idea of giving to pressure for release has been building in his mind since he was first put in a bosal. It is one of the cornerstones of the whole training program.

The ask-and-release keeps the horse collected and leaves his head in the proper position to maintain balance. So does the second thing to remember: keeping your hands low when putting pressure on the bit. Many riders lift their hands to their chests to back their horses. This doesn't encourage a horse to yield his jaw and keep his head down. A high hand lifts his jaw and opens his mouth. Both actions, because they cause the horse pain, are serious faults in backing.

With proper preparation beforehand, maybe one horse in twenty-five has trouble understanding what his rider wants. If this is the case, there are at least three ways to make backing clearer to him:

1. As long as the horse's problem is *not* throwing his head (or body) in the air, halt him on the rail. Have a friend stand in front of the horse. As you ask with the reins, your friend can tap or push the horse on the chest to move him backward *along the rail.*

2. If you have to work alone, dismount and stand beside the horse, holding the reins in your hand. Give him the rein signal from the ground and tap his chest with your free hand.

3. A third method is to tie the stirrups together and attach long lines to the horse's bit. Pass them through the stirrups and line-drive the horse backward. While someone taps the horse from the front, you stand behind him and give and take with the long lines.

Any of these methods is good as long as you are producing this backward motion. It is a hard motion for a horse to pick up if he hasn't been prepared, but if the trainer has done the groundwork, the horse should not become confused.

In order to refine the back, the horse has to know the basics of side-passing or at least be able to move away from leg pressure. If your hands control the horse's forehand and regulate the horse's speed, it is your legs that control the horse's hindquarters and create the

speed. The practical application of this principle usually comes up in your first horse show, when the horse next to you gets in your way while you are trying to back your horse. To put your horse in a safe, uncluttered position to back up and avoid a collision, push his body to the left with your right leg or to the right with your left leg *(photo 15)*. Hold him in place, with both legs giving equal pressure. This way you are using your legs to create motion but also to steer your horse without having to rely on the reins alone.

When backing, don't use your legs to ask for any more speed than is necessary to move backward smoothly. In Western Riding and Western Reining, one of the worst things you can do is back up too fast. It frightens the horse. No matter how well-trained he is, if he is backed at speed he is going to open his mouth a little. He won't commit this serious fault if he is backed slowly and smoothly. A judge should respect this, and if your horse backs nicely, he'll give you a few extra points for it.

These extra points don't come easily, though. Backing, whether for Pleasure class, Trail class, Western Riding, or Reining, is a thing you have to practice each day. Each time you work your horse, back him a few steps. When you are finished working him for the day, back him again and then stop and sit quietly. Back three or four more steps, stop, and let him relax.

5. SIDE-PASSING

When the horse is carrying his bit easily and backing on signal, he is ready to learn side-passing. By this time he is flexing and giving his head to the right and left *(photo 16)*. He isn't particularly sharp—he is still trotting off into his canter—but side-passing will make the young horse's sides more sensitive, thus improving his canter departure. Side-passing allows the rider's cues to become lighter but more effective. With the additional head control, the horse will drop back into the bridle and improve in balance.

Remember, before teaching the horse something new, always warm him up by repeating the old lessons, things he already knows. This increases his confidence, in himself and in the trainer, in addition to building good habits.

To keep this young horse calm and confident, I want to make side-passing as easy as possible for him. The less confusion and the fewer fights, the faster he will learn. I begin by dismounting and turning the horse's hindquarters to the wall or rail of the arena so he can't back out of position. For the time being, I'll only work him in one direction. (Generally I work from the right to the left, because this seems to be

51

easier for the majority of horses.) From the ground, I take hold of the reins and turn the horse's head slightly to the right—away from the direction he will move *(photo 17)*. With my free hand I tap him behind the girth where my foot would normally rest. Another way is to use a dressage whip or longe whip and tap the horse on the hindquarters with it. The reason I sometimes use a whip here is that I can't reach his hindquarters with my hand and there are some horses who tend to let their hindquarters swing out instead of holding their bodies straight. The whip is simply the way you control the horse's hindquarters from the ground. It is never used to beat the horse down the wall or to see if he can be made to run sideways.

As the horse begins to take a step or two to the left, I continue to hold his head slightly to the right. This is the beginning of his lead change as well as of teaching him the head and body position for side movement. At this point I'm not worried about how he is moving his feet. It may be a ragged movement and it may look clumsy, but I will be satisfied with *any* motion sideways. If the basic motion is correct, the finesse will come and he will begin to cross his right feet over his left as he moves to the side. I tap the horse and let him take two or three steps. Then I let him stop and rest and gather his wits. After a minute or two I'll ask for a few more steps and then rest him again. In three to five days, working for about 5 minutes a day, he should be able to side-pass the length of the arena wall. Only when he is working well from right to left do I begin all over again, side-passing from left to right.

16

17

By teaching this movement first from the ground, I eliminate a lot of confusion for the horse. I'm holding his head so he can't walk forward. The arena wall or rail holds his hindquarters in place so he can't back up. The whip is keeping him from going to the right and at the same time is asking him to move to the left.

A mounted side pass is just a refinement of this exercise. After warming up the horse at his usual walk, trot, and canter both ways of the ring, I take him to the rail and face him to it, turning his head slightly to the right. If he starts forward, the rail—not my hands—will hold him in place. With a long whip in my right hand, I tap him on the hindquarters and squeeze my right leg on the girth, hoping to get some movement to the left. I may have to overcompensate for a tighter rein to keep him from walking down the rail and out of his side pass. Just as before, I am more concerned at the moment with correct motion than with finesse. If the horse takes a few steps sideways, I'll stop and let him rest awhile.

At this time I am creating a stop on a side pass and also instilling in my horse the idea of stop as a reward. I find that most trainers don't reward their horses enough. I know I didn't when I was young. Amateurs, however, reward their horses enough but often at the wrong time. For instance, when I am teaching a rider to change leads and the horse cheats him flagrantly, perhaps taking advantage of the rider's inexperience, I have seen the rider stop right there and pat the horse. This is not the time to reward the horse. This is the time to use your legs and move him into that gait and make him do it right.

My reward is a little different, too. I do pat my horses, especially at a show, during a tough Trail class, or when we've been working at something and the horse finally gets the idea. I'll stop and pat him real hard. But usually my reward is to let my horse stop and sit. When I let him stop and breathe, this is his relaxation. Soon he learns that a chance to rest is his reward for doing the job right.

When I stop a horse, I do it by saying "Whoa" and dropping my rein hand firmly on his withers. I sit there for a few minutes and then raise my hand and side-pass him a few steps farther. This is one of my basics. When I drop my hand and rest it on the horse's withers, the horse knows he can stop and relax. I don't lift my hand until I want him to move.

This halting and side-passing goes on for about three to five days in each direction, just like the groundwork. As in the groundwork, I don't ask for a side pass from right to left until the horse can do it well from left to right. I practice side-passing only for about 5 minutes a day, and then only when the horse has been warmed up and is ready to concentrate. On the average, a young horse should be side-passing well, the length of the arena and without the aid of a whip, in two weeks.

After each day's work I continue to tie the horse around for a few minutes—both ways—in his stall. I usually use the bitting rig I have made with the saddle and bridle. Tightening the reins only a fraction of an inch each day, I will work up to a 25- or 30-degree lateral flexion (bend) at the most.

As the horse's sides become more sensitive, I practice some variations on the side pass. I try it the width of the arena without the aid of the wall or rail. I try two-tracking at the trot. (Two-tracking, when *I* speak of it, is a side pass with a little forward motion. The horse slants across the ring instead of going straight across it. A dressage rider would more likely call it leg-yielding.)

At this point the horse is ready to begin working with a gate, which is yet another variation on the side pass. Opening and shutting a gate is a movement that crops up in many Western horse show classes, even though it is hardly ever used in real ranch or trail work. The Western Riding class pattern usually includes a gate and the Trail Horse classes always feature one.

After being bitted in the stall, the horse has learned the rudiments of backing. He has learned to give to the bit and yield his jaw to its pressure, and he may even back away from it in the stall. He has been taught backing under saddle, so he is now ready to put backing and side-passing together.

After warming up my horse, I walk up to the gate and halt the horse parallel to it. I rest my hand on his withers to hold the halt and let him settle. (Don't try to walk up to the gate and push it open in one movement. This is where many people get into trouble. They look upon the gate as a timed event. They rush their horses through it off-balance and nervous.)

When the horse is settled I unlatch the gate and push it open *(photo 18)*. As it swings open, I back the horse a few steps and let my hand slide along the top of the gate *(photo 19)*. The reason I move back to push the gate open, instead of pushing it at the end, is that I have more control over it nearer the hinge

18

19

20

21

and because it is easier to move from this position. I side-pass the horse into the gate to push it open.

Now I walk up the gate—letting it slide through my hand again—and halt. (When I work the gate I keep the horse walking forward until his hindquarters are past it.) Then I rest a second. I turn the horse around the gate *(photo 20)*, stop, and rest when he is through it. I then side-pass him back to push the gate closed *(photo 21)*. I fasten the gate and stop once more. When the gate is closed and latched, I drop my rein hand on the horse's neck as before, but this time I'll let him sit for perhaps 15 seconds to get his bearings. Only then do I move on to something else.

6. MOVING OUT

It is a fact of any horse trainer's life that colts, like children, learn their lessons faster indoors than outdoors. In an indoor arena there are fewer distractions and fewer variables like weather and ground surface. At the training stable where I do my work, these are big considerations, since we do most of our green-breaking in the winter when an indoor arena is not just a luxury, but a necessity.

If you live in a mild climate or have been training your horse in the summer, you probably haven't had to resort to an indoor arena. As long as the surface of the ring is smooth, with a good cushion, and the fencing is smooth and solid, an outdoor ring is just as good and sometimes a lot more pleasant than an indoor one.

But if riding rings promote concentration and discipline in horses, it is equally true that arenas, either indoor or outdoor, eventually become pretty boring places for both horses and riders. Before that point I begin to look for new ways to test my horse's progress and keep him fresh and interested. These new areas are horse shows and cross-country trails, and their value isn't just as a testing ground. Outside work keeps any horse fresh and happy in his work, and providing this variety is one of the most important jobs of the performance horse trainer.

The horse's basic training has taken about three months of working at least five days a week. If the horse is quiet, I try to give him more outside work at this time. Once he knows his basics, it makes a nice change for him, and besides, he is ready to be schooled outside where there are more distractions. If his training has taken place indoors, the young horse isn't always ready for actual trail riding at this time. Many horses, especially if they have been trained inside, just don't know at first what is wanted in the open fields. They get confused, and the riders end up jerking and fighting their horses because they can't get them to cross a stream or go past some strange obstacle. If the young horse is shown too much too soon outdoors, this work will mess him up more than it will help him.

At the same time, even the best young horses are pretty squirrelly the first day outdoors if all their training has been carried out indoors. With such a horse, I often wonder if I've even trained him at all when I take him outside. The first time in a ring or pasture under saddle, he is going to forget everything he has learned. He will look at everything and not pay much attention to his cues. No matter how disgusted I am at this point, I find that now is the time to say calmly, "Okay, settle down." I stop the horse from bouncing around and work with him patiently. I don't exhaust him, though. I've got this horse's confidence, and I don't want to shake it. I just ride him in an outdoor riding ring. After two or three days the novelty of the great outdoors has worn off and he is paying attention to me. If I'm willing to hold my temper through this period of adjustment, I'll get a lot more done than if I really have it out with him the first day. Then I can do what the rider who has been training outdoors can do a little earlier: take him out on the trails, walk him over logs, side-pass him around bushes—get him used to the old routine in a new place. If all the basic training has been done in an outdoor ring, I will probably need to spend less time just riding around and getting the young horse used to the wide open spaces.

After warming up my horse I'll start two-tracking him. I may trot the horse in an open field, side-pass a few strides, and then let him go forward into a two-tracking motion. He is moving away from the rider's leg, going forward on a slant *(photo 22)*. I might have to take hold of his mouth a little more firmly outside. I might have to turn his head a little more to hold him in motion, because he'll want to look around at things. I'll work on the side pass at the trot. In short, I'll keep him fresh and interested.

At this point, after some outdoor work, I'll give the horse a vacation. Where a lot of amateurs spoil their horses is the constant walk, trot, canter, walk, trot, canter, on the rail, on the rail, on the rail. You can sour them even before they have been bitted. It happens especially with young show prospects. So many yearling halter horses are brushed to death. Their legs are wrapped before they are even completely formed. I get them for training, and they are already the sourest animals around. Riding helps to some extent, but they will always be sour and foul and unwilling to learn because they've been pestered constantly as young colts. They've never had any free time to themselves. They've been constantly shown, picked at, and posed.

This is another reason to back off a horse and give him a break instead of pushing him right into showing. He knows his basics, and he has worked pretty hard. I don't turn the young horses out completely, because they can get into too poor a condition if one bullies the others away from the feed racks. Instead, I turn them out during the day, giving them some exercise on their own, and then I bring them in at night. That way I make sure they are getting enough to eat and can check them every day. I do a minimum of brushing at this time. Ordinarily a horse likes to be clean, but during this time I find a horse would rather be left rough. His mind has been strained. He has been in intensive training and has learned things he never thought existed. He thought he was going to graze and play all his life. Schooling has been a shock to him, and like any hardworking student he needs a vacation, mentally and physically. That's why I turn him out with his friends and let him be a horse. Feed him, give him good food, keep him healthy, but otherwise just leave your horse alone for a while.

How long this vacation lasts depends on the individual case. I let most young horses rest a month, until show season. If there isn't enough time, two weeks will have to do. Any break in the action is what a young horse in training needs here.

When a horse takes his leads, backs, side passes, flexes, and bends right and left, I consider him a green-broke horse. Although I am looking forward to Western Riding and Western Reining classes, when he begins his show career I want to make each of my horses into a good, basic pleasure horse. In this case, the goal is part of the training program. The training of many horses often stops right here. Maybe their owners don't want to do

Western Riding or Reining, maybe they don't want their horses to compete, maybe a number of things.

But if your horse is to be shown in competition, I'd start at little shows. I would enter my green-broke horse in Pleasure, Halter, and Equitation classes until I was satisfied—not by the number of ribbons he won but by his general attitude and behavior—that he was not afraid of anything connected with showing. He would learn to load in the trailer and haul to shows. He would go into classes, and after three or four times around the ring he would be calm and ready for work. He would tie to the trailer and stand tied. If he won something, fine, but what I'd be concerned with is schooling the horse at these little shows . . . for future shows.

Is it possible to show a young horse too much? If he is being worked five days a week, showing on two of those days won't tax him. Ten weekends isn't too much to ask, as long as he is limited to Pleasure, Equitation, and Halter classes. When he begins his advanced training, your horse is going to need the background and confidence that this showing will give him.

After a few shows, the horse may begin to get bored with the routine. He may act a little dull, or if he is usually spooky he'll just start acting like a well-mannered horse. This is the time to start him on something more challenging. Just as we moved him outdoors to keep him from being bored with indoor work, just as we took him trail-riding, just as we entered him in shows, so we are going to start training this horse for advanced work to expand his mind and keep him interested. I certainly don't start putting a spin or rollback on my horse now, but I do start him on his lead changes.

FOR
WESTERN RIDING
AND REINING:
ADVANCED WORK

7. LEAD CHANGING

Like dressage tests, the object of training for the Western Riding class is not to teach the pattern itself (see page 138) but to teach the movements the horse needs to perform the pattern. At this point your horse already knows how to work the gate and how to back straight, so lead changing is the next thing he needs to learn.

As everyone reading this book probably knows, lead changing in the stock-seat performance horse is what dressage riders would call a flying lead change—that is, it is made at the canter, at the moment of suspension when the horse's four feet are off the ground. (The dressage term "flying" is misleading in suggesting speed. This movement is always done slowly.) It requires more athletic ability than the simple change at the trot or the walk, and mastering it makes the performance horse that much more graceful and versatile. So when I talk of changing leads here, I'm talking of changing leads and shifting balance in midair.

Teaching a horse to change leads is very difficult. Even correctly *asking* a trained horse to change leads is a knack a lot of people never learn. If you haven't had someone explain it to you, it's going to be very hard for you to teach your horse to do it. Riders must also be able to recognize leads right off. If you are unsure about your own knowledge and coordination, this is one point where you might want to seek a professional trainer's advice.

Lead changing is too crucial to go at it in a hit-or-miss fashion. If the horse is off-balance he can mess himself up completely. If he gets to dropping his shoulder and not catching his hind lead (cross-firing), it is very hard to break him of the habit. Another thing to consider is that there are riders as well as horses who are not natural lead changers and, like horses with the same problem, they need special attention to master it.

So amateur trainers have to know their limitations. Maybe a rider has a good seat but poor hands. Some people have difficulty recognizing correct leads. If you have any problems along these lines, keep in mind that you have put a lot of work into this horse and be careful not to blow it all through too much pride.

One of the most important things to keep in mind is that a Western Riding lead change is slow and controlled. The horse is held upright and in balance. He is not thrown over onto the other lead by the reins alone. Keeping this in mind, before I even ask for the lead change I watch the young horse, study his conformation, and note whether he is a natural lead changer. If he *is* a natural, if he automatically changes leads when he is in the pasture, then my only problem will be to put him in a natural, balanced position to change leads in an arena. If the horse is not a natural lead changer, I will do the same thing but I'll also have to make my cues very plain to make sure he gets the idea. With this kind of horse I can take nothing for granted, leave nothing to his personal judgment.

In giving a horse these plain cues, I don't want to use

spurs. The tendency to use them too strongly will make the horse bolt forward. If he is jabbed at every lead change, the horse will get into the habit of jumping forward, away from the rider's leg. This will make him lose his balance, his collection, and his calm attitude.

Remember that, along with the extra control of the horse's head and body, flexion and two-tracking have been preparing the horse for the lead change. This ability to hold his body straight and upright while moving away from the rider's leg is essential for an upright, balanced lead change (*photo 23*). And the lead change must be upright. It must he a movement of only the horse's legs, not the throwing of his whole forehand to the left or right.

As in all Western riding, positioning is everything when changing leads. Particularly in the beginning, I want to leave my horse a wide margin for error and make lead changing as easy as I can for him. So after warming him up as usual with plenty of work on two-tracking and side-passing, I begin to canter him in a semicircle roughly half the size of the arena in which I'm working. This in itself is hard for many advanced riders because they are used to riding in full circles. The semicircle's straight side bisects the arena. In other words, I canter a curve close to the arena walls on the short side and then cut across the ring on a straight line.

The straight line is where I will ask for a lead change (*photo 24*). There are a lot of advantages to this. It's easier to hold the horse upright on a straight line. If I ask for a change the instant the horse is straight, he has the entire length of the line to give me the change. (If he hasn't taken the lead, I have two or three more strides to ask him again or, if he hasn't caught his hind lead, he has a few more strides to pick it up.)

23
24

Especially when first teaching lead changes, be careful not to wait until the horse gets to the opposite wall and then try to *throw* the horse onto the other lead by use of the reins alone. Not only does this throw him off-balance, it gets him into the habit of cutting his corners in anticipation. Another way to avoid anticipation is to canter the semicircle several times before asking for a lead change. It helps relax the horse and discourages him from rushing toward his corners.

Besides when and where to ask for a lead change, keep in mind *how* to ask for one. I start with a light rein contact, with the reins in both hands. After cantering a few semicircles, I choose a time when the horse is relaxed, upright on the straight line, and not too close to either wall. Then I side-pass him a step at the canter to put him on the opposite lead. I am careful to hold my weight steady and not throw the reins at the horse. When I feel him change leads, I still hold him upright and continue on the straight line until I reach the wall. Then I turn him to begin semicircling the other half of the arena.

This is one of the few things in riding that are easier to describe than to do. The cues are the same as those of the side pass. To change from the right lead onto the left, for instance, I bring the left rein against the horse's neck and push with my right leg. At first I am very obvious about sitting straight and not leaning forward, and if I am asking for a change onto the right lead, I put weight on my left hip and push with my left leg just as I would if I were asking the horse to side-pass at the trot or walk.

For many people this is an entirely new way of asking for a lead change, and though they can understand it mentally, it takes a while for them to get the knack of it physically. It's something my students have to find out for themselves. It takes a few tries for both horse and rider to get it, but once they do, it's a very simple, logical way to ask for a lead change.

Holding your weight steady is important. If you throw your weight forward, you throw your horse off-balance. If you ask for a change on a curve instead of on a straight line, the horse's head and body are thrown in opposite directions. Because his hindquarters don't have a chance to catch up with his forehand, the horse stays upright the only way he can—by cross-firing.

Once the horse is changing easily, I can begin variations on lead changes. These variations are nothing more or less than the Western Riding pattern. The object of this is to put the lead change, not the pattern, on the horse's mind. The cones, pylons, or barrels that are set up on the Western Riding course are only signposts that will help the horse and rider measure the course and know when to change leads, just as the letters mark a dressage arena. Although barrels work well for this, it is a good idea to invest in regulation Day-Glo pylons if you plan to have your horse compete in Western Riding classes. If he works with the pylons every day, he won't be startled by them when he sees them at a horse show.

The exercise I use in preparing the young horse for Western Riding competition has eight steps. After I have set up eight pylons and the log in the regulation pattern, my first step is to put the horse into a slow, free-moving canter and circle the number 1 pylon several times (*diagram A*). I say circle, but what I really want is an oval with a flattened side. A truly round circle would not give the horse the straight line he needs to change his lead. I canter around the pylon as many times as it takes to relax the horse, then I ask for the lead change on the straight

DIAGRAM A

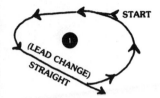

8

3   7 ▱▱▱▱
         LOG

2

4

5   6

75

DIAGRAM B

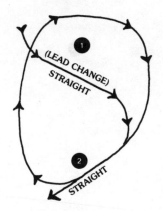

(LEAD CHANGE)
STRAIGHT

STRAIGHT

8

3

7 ▨▨▨▨
LOG

4

5   6

76

DIAGRAM C

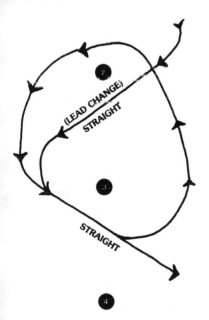

(LEAD CHANGE)

STRAIGHT

STRAIGHT

LOG

77

DIAGRAM D

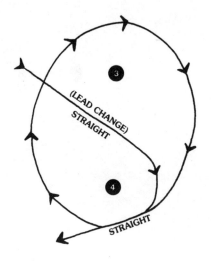

STRAIGHT

(LEAD CHANGE)
STRAIGHT

LOG

78

DIAGRAM E

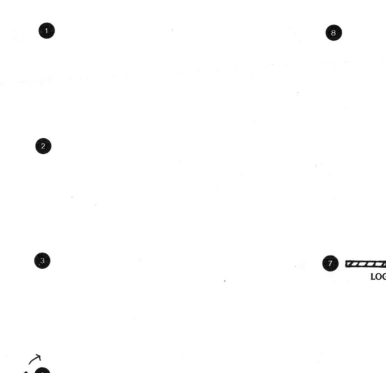

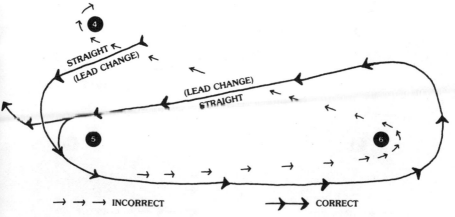

DIAGRAM F

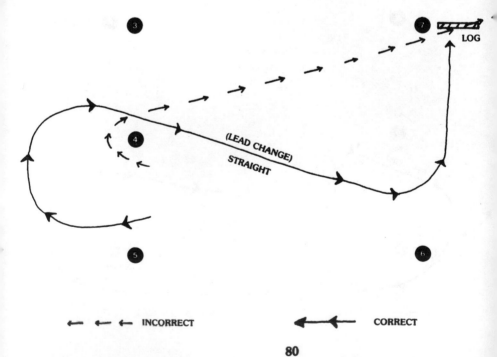

(LEAD CHANGE)

STRAIGHT

LOG

← ← ← INCORRECT   ← ← CORRECT

80

DIAGRAM G

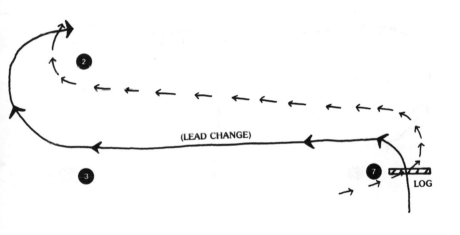

(LEAD CHANGE)

LOG

← ← ← **INCORRECT**   ◄—◄— **CORRECT**

81

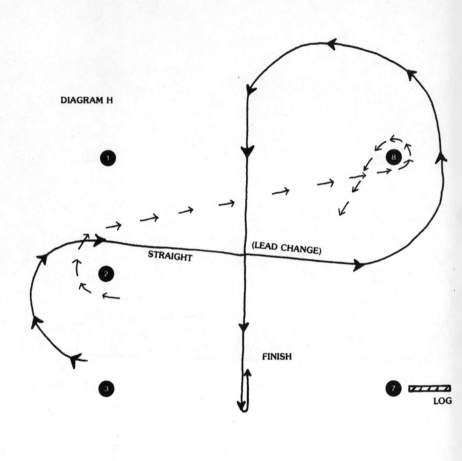

DIAGRAM H

STRAIGHT (LEAD CHANGE)

FINISH

LOG

← ← ← INCORRECT   ← ← CORRECT

82

line. The horse may drift out quite a ways on this line before he can begin circling pylons 2 and 1, which is the next step. I let him drift if he needs to because I want to avoid creating any tension in him here. At this point, all I'm concerned with is a lead change and correct movement.

With the change of lead, I head for pylon 2 (diagram B). Again the horse may have a tendency to drift out on his first turn around pylon 2, but I continue on back around pylon 1 and circle both pylons several times, relaxing the horse and correcting my straight line.

In the third step of my exercise (diagram C), the horse again changes lead on the straight line and moves on around pylon 3. Again there will be the tendency to drift out, and I circle pylons 3 and 2 several times to relax the horse and straighten the line to prepare him to change leads for the fourth step.

I repeat the same process for circling pylons 4 and 3 (diagram D).

My next step will involve again changing leads on the straight line and moving around pylon 5 and across the pattern to pylon 6 (diagram E).

I know it's important to give myself plenty of room in circling the pylons—I'm not talking about the tight circles used in barrel racing. In Western Riding I want to run the circles in a manner that will keep my horse upright at all times so that he can change leads freely.

As shown in diagram E, I move around pylon 6, and head back toward pylon 5—both for relaxation and for getting into position for the next step, which involves pylons 4 and 7. The reason I move toward pylon 5 is that when I change leads I'm changing from left to right; unless I compensate for the horse's tendency to move too directly toward pylon 4, I will be thrown out of position for pylon 7 and the log.

As I move toward pylon 7 *(diagram F)*, changing leads midway, I actually head in the direction of pylon 6, which will allow me time to straighten the horse and approach the log head on.

After my horse has cantered over the log, he can move freely and in proper position toward pylon 3 *(diagram G)*.

With my lead change in the middle, I'll have the room to maneuver in an upright manner around pylon 2, moving back toward pylon 7 and changing lead midway *(diagram H)*. Then I'm in position to make a wide turn, my horse still upright, around pylon 8. I continue on a straight line *at the same gait and speed,* moving ten feet past the center of the arena. This allows me to back up the required ten feet and finish the pattern at the correct spot in the arena, midway between pylons 3 and 7.

It's important to remember that Western Riding is not a speed event. The faster you try to do the pattern, the faster you will land in trouble.

When the horse is ready to begin competing in Western Riding classes, he will have to practice the pattern as it will be ridden at the show (see The Appaloosa example, page 138), just as a good dressage horse has to go through his test several times. He shouldn't practice it so many times that he begins to memorize it and anticipate every move—not so many times that he begins to sour on the whole idea—but two or three times as an exercise before the competition. Other than these few practice drills, it's better to practice parts of the pattern rather than repeat the whole thing over and over.

When I work the whole pattern I pay particular attention to the first lead. It must be picked up on the center line; if it isn't, the whole pattern falls apart very quickly. To put my horse in the best position to pick up this lead, I keep him collected and angle him slightly toward the wall of the arena, away from the pattern. If his head is a little toward the outside when I cue him, the horse will be pushed onto the outside—which will free his inside hind leg to pick up the correct lead.

No matter how nervous you may be, fight the urge to race for the first pylon and get everything over with in a hurry. Give the horse room to bend and keep his balance. Go wide around your pylons and give him plenty of room to prepare himself. Use the whole arena. That's what it's there for.

The log is another feature of the Western Riding pattern that many beginners want to rush. Walk into the arena, work the gate calmly, and give the horse a few seconds to collect his wits. Walk straight to the log and aim the horse for the center of it. If the young horse stops and looks at the log, just calmly squeeze his sides with your legs—don't flail him with them—and push him on over it gently and smoothly. In every Western Riding pattern, the horse is supposed to trot on the other side of the log. In other words, the horse is supposed to walk across the log and *then* pick up the trot. Don't rush this. If the horse barely crosses the log and is asked to trot immediately, he quickly begins anticipating, and soon he is trotting before he gets to the log and then jumping the log. I avoid this by walking over the log, taking three or four steps at the walk, and then easing the horse out into a jog.

Western Riding class demands what amounts to an advanced dressage horse, a highly trained athlete. Not every horse can do a Western Riding pattern, and not every horse can do it under the stress of competition. However, if a horse has a natural lead change or a rider who is willing to work with him to develop one, this is a class that can prepare him for even more advanced work. It increases the value of a pleasure horse and complements a Western Reining horse.

So many reining-horse trainers make their horses reining horses exclusively and refuse to allow them to do anything else for fear of spoiling them. Nothing is likely to spoil them less than Western Riding. In fact, I believe that if they would enter their reining horses in Western Riding and compete in these classes as well as in reining, they would find that the horse improves in attitude as well as performance. Western Riding demands a calm, balanced, and athletic horse. It doesn't demand a fast one. From Western Pleasure and Equitation classes, I think Western Riding is the next logical step in training a prospective Western Reining horse, or any other that has the mental and physical ability for advanced work.

8. ABOUT REINING

Reining is possibly the Western performance horse's greatest challenge. Like advanced dressage, reining calls for great strength, good timing, and extensive training, and like dressage, Reining classes vary in difficulty and in pattern. The first level is Hackamore Reining, where the horses are ridden in a bosal. Then there is Junior Reining, which is open to horses four years old or younger. Depending on the class description, these horses will be shown in a bosal or a bit. The highest level is Senior Reining, which is open to bitted horses five years and older. Breed associations, 4H, and most open horse shows sponsor Reining classes, which can be restricted to registered horses or open to virtually any horse and rider who cares to enter.

Until recently, reining was more or less a professional event that few amateurs and their horses dared to enter. Cutting was the event that attracted advanced amateurs who wanted something more than Western Pleasure and Halter classes. But with more and more sophisticated and talented riders coming up from the youth divisions, with more clinics being given by prominent reining-horse trainers, and with the initiation of the amateur Reining classes, reining horses and reining competitions became the coming thing for advanced stock-seat riders, whether amateur or professional.

Reining today has a lot going for it. It is something you can work at alone. It needs little special equipment or props. It has the excitement of cutting, but you don't have to maintain cattle or find another person for the team-roping event.

Reining also attracts a certain kind of rider, a person who is interested in horsemanship as an art and a science. Such a person realizes there is more to riding a horse than yank and spur and wants to learn the finer points. It's the same mentality that sends hunt-seat riders into dressage and eventing. They too are looking for something more demanding than walk-trot-canter-reverse around the arena. For the stock-seat rider, Western Riding and Western Reining provide this challenge.

To be successful in reining, you must be able to concentrate under pressure, both in the training arena *and* in the show ring. When riding a reining horse you must know where the horse's feet are every minute. You must know if your horse is balanced, and, if he is not, how to get him balanced. You cannot just sit there on your horse and admire the scenery. When you go into that ring, you've got to have collection on your horse and on your mind.

Admittedly, some people don't have the physical coordination needed for training a reining horse. They can't react fast enough or they just don't have the mind for it. There's no disgrace in not being able to train a reining horse, and it doesn't mean you can't own one just because you didn't "do it yourself." There are a lot of good amateur riders who can take a trained reining horse and have a lot of fun with him. It is my business to produce these horses so people can take them, compete with them, and have a good time with them. A well-trained horse can teach you a lot. If you haven't worked with a professional horse trainer, you should, for this is the best way to get a start in reining. With a well-trained horse you can learn what the correct movement *feels* like as well as what it looks like. You can change leads, spin, and stop a horse that knows his job and can forgive a few errors on the part of the rider.

Many people are reluctant to get on a made reining horse for fear they will ruin him. An equally great number of professional trainers prey on their clients' lack of confidence: "Don't ever ride the horse unless I'm there to tell you what to do" or "Keep him here at the barn instead of taking him home, otherwise he'll probably get messed up." If the horse has been well trained, if he is sensible, and if the rider is sensible, the horse is not going to unlearn everything he knows or go mad. Once in a while both horse and rider might need a tune-up—a few lessons with a professional to sharpen them up—but a correctly trained horse is not going to fall apart at the least suggestion.

If you have the experience, the time, and the patience to take your horse on to Western Reining, the next question to ask is whether you have the horse for it. You will notice that as we've brought the young horse along, versatility has been emphasized. We started the horse as a Western Pleasure horse suitable for Western Equitation and Halter classes. He progressed to Western Riding. Versatility is something I believe in and something I stress with my clients. I enter other classes besides reining with my reining horses, and you surely want to enter more than one class as well. The typical amateur wants to enter

Western Pleasure, Western Riding, Trail class—and horses I train for riding should have these skills. A horse I would buy for reining should be able to enter other classes, and I would encourage him to compete in them.

It's not unreasonable to expect a good reining horse to be versatile. He is a superb athlete, and when you ask him to do a variety of things, you're not ruining him but improving him. A pleasure horse doesn't always have what it takes to be a good reining horse, but a good reining horse, if he has had good basic training, can be an adequate pleasure horse. Just like the decathlon champion, he can do two things well, one thing super, and several things adequately, but he has had to master all of them.

This insistence on versatility also helps a reining horse's attitude. It helps him stay fresh for a good long time. Most amateur riders want to show their horses. If there is a show every weekend, they go. If reining is the only thing their horse knows how to do, they'll rein that horse every weekend and burn him out. But if your horse has been brought along as I've described so far, you can give him a rest from reining and still compete with him. He can enter reining once or twice a month and enter other classes in between. Then when a big show comes along, you can get your horse tuned up—or tune him up yourself—and be very competitive.

There is another argument for bringing a horse along with an eye to versatility. Since not all horses have what it takes to be reining horses, if your horse has been prepared for nothing but reining and then fails at that, all your time and money have been wasted. But if he has been brought along sensibly, he may not have the ability to do spins and sliding stops—and therefore no future as a reining horse—but he can still be an excellent Western riding or pleasure horse. If a horse doesn't have the ability to be a reining horse, I don't try to force that on him, and I certainly wouldn't advise an amateur to try it. I would suggest we do something else with him. No one can make a silk purse out of anything but silk, and if the horse hasn't got what it takes to make a reining horse, his trainer can still be proud of producing a very good performance horse for other classes.

It isn't easy to ride a reining pattern or produce a reining horse, although the object of the game is to make it look easy. There is an overall impression a rider wants to create with a horse, a certain look and style to give the reining patterns. For instance, although a reining horse is a little freer moving than a Western Riding horse, a reining horse should never work too fast, wide open. Occasionally you see riders asking for nothing but speed from their horses. It is sometimes called Texas style and comes from dealing with roping horses. Their stop is a roping stop, in my opinion, not a reining stop.

To me, reining is separate from roping or even Western Riding. A good reining pattern is pretty. Every movement is precise and neat and exactly what is called for. There is nothing flamboyant about it. The horse is not jerked to a stop; he flows into it. If the pattern calls for a sliding stop, the horse runs in and puts it down and acts like he *wants* to come to a sliding stop. A reining pattern is just right. It's just there. It's poetry in motion.

9. SPINS AND ROLLBACKS

A spin is a pirouette, a 360-degree or more turn on the horse's hindquarters, and it is usually performed at speed. The horse plants his inside hind foot and, maintaining the left lead, spins to the left. Spinning to the right, he maintains his right lead. While spinning on this hind pivot foot, the horse shifts his weight toward his hindquarters and lets his front feet cross each other just as he did in the side pass.

When the horse is changing leads easily, he is usually ready to start learning to spin. But not always. I do run into horses that can't handle the strain physically even though their basic training has equipped them to handle it mentally. In spite of having the coordination to change leads and side-pass, spinning may be too physically exhausting and straining at this time. The horse's legs can't take the strain.

So even if you are quite sure your horse is ready to spin, have him x-rayed and examined by a good race-track veterinarian who knows horses' legs and the strain they can safely take, not by your local practitioner. The racetrack vet will be able to tell you if your horse is ready for this kind of training. Because I hold to this practice, my horses don't have a lot of leg problems. The older horses I'm really working do get wind-puffs. I have had some bog spavins. But I have never lamed a horse or had a horse break down on me, so I feel the precautions are worth the time and expense.

Another thing I've learned from racetrack veterinarians and found to be true is that it is not a good idea to wrap a horse's legs with bandages and braces before they are needed. A wash or skin bracer for aching muscles is fine, but as far as Western horses go, wrapping the legs over a wash of Absorbine will only blister the horse unnecessarily Leave the horse's legs alone. If a problem develops, *then* treat it, but strong bracers under bandages is not preventive medicine. It won't keep your horse from ever having leg problems any more than taking an aspirin when you're feeling fine will keep you from ever getting a headache.

This is not to say I don't protect my horses' legs in training. I do. I use splint boots on every horse I train, no matter how straight he travels. When he is learning spins and rollbacks, a horse can trip over himself or forget where his feet are and step on himself. I also always use a breast collar to hold the saddle firmly in place and a sheepskin cover over the girth to prevent girth galls. I carry a bat instead of wearing spurs, because I don't want to ask for speed until the horse is ready to deliver it. It's too easy to give the horse a leg cue inadvertently when he's learning to spin, and spurs can just compound the error.

After equipment, the second thing to consider is the method you will use to teach the horse to spin. Various trainers have various methods. Whatever works for them is fine, but like everybody else, I have my own way of doing things. It certainly isn't the only way, but it works for me.

For instance, I don't like to teach a horse to spin in an open field. Outdoors there are too many distractions, too many causes of confusion, and too many ways for the horse to avoid doing what I ask. When a horse resists his rider, he gets punished. Outdoors it is easier for the horse to become confused and resist. Pretty soon the horse is so upset and so scared of getting whipped or spurred that he doesn't know which direction to go. A lot of reining horses turn around or spin out of fear. I want my horses to turn around out of training and coordination. I want my horse to understand what I want quickly and calmly, so I teach him any new movement indoors and away from distractions.

Although the arena wall is a good training aid in teaching the horse to side-pass, it's pretty limited when you are teaching him to spin. Some trainers like it, but the only thing I ever got out of running a horse down the long side and turning him into the wall to reverse was teaching the horse to look for a wall and *depend* on it to turn around. If you can start your horse this way, that's wonderful, but it doesn't work for me. If you begin turning your horse to the wall from a trot, which some trainers recommend, you'll have to spank him pretty hard because he's not going to be too eager to turn toward a wall, even if you are three feet away from it.

There is also a tendency to jerk the horse's head around *(photo 25)*, and in doing that you jerk the horse on his front end. This forces the horse's weight onto the forehand and off-balance. Strung out like this, the horse bolts out of his turn or falls out of it, instead of working off

his hindquarters. With these things going against him, it will take the horse a long time to figure out what you want him to do and then to do it right.

I want to start my horse turning around without making him jump forward from the bat or jump to the side from the spur to the shoulder. I want to give him the idea of turning without scaring him to death. I want him to get this idea quickly, without confusion and without a fight. There is nothing particularly valuable about a fight; it sure doesn't help the horse learn any easier or enjoy his work more.

Because of this philosophy of training, and because of an abundance of box stalls with dirt floors and shavings for bedding, I've developed what might be called the stock-seat rider's version of the British Hitchcock pen or jumping lane. Both work on the idea of putting a horse where he has to do what is asked because he has no other option. A jumping lane is a narrow fenced lane with jumps across it. The horse has to take the jumps as he moves down the lane, because there is no other way to go. He doesn't become confused and run out. In the same way I use a box stall to teach a horse to spin. He has to work correctly off his hindquarters because that is the only path he can follow.

Depending on the lightness of the horse, I may want to go back to the iron bosal with or without a tie-down while he is learning to spin. With this or the snaffle on, I walk the horse—mounted—into a box stall. (It isn't a big stall, just 10 feet square.) Once in there, with the door open, I walk him around the edges of the stall for a few minutes each day as part of his training. For three days or so I continue this to give the horse the general idea, to get him used to moving in a small circle, and to let him see where he is going. Soon he knows the area he is to travel and its limitations. He becomes confident and gives his head when I put pressure on the bit or bosal, because he has already mastered the five basic movements we spoke of earlier. Gradually I start to pull him into smaller and smaller circles to start the basis of his spin.

At this point a lot of people make a mistake. They try to draw the horse's head almost to their own knee. They have a tendency to pull the horse's head out of the balance point, which is *straight ahead.* One reason I tied the horse around to both sides was to make him supple. Because he is now limber and flexible, I hope he'll be able to hold his head straight when he has to, as well as turn it.

Now the upcoming word is the most important one in all horse training: *motion.* When I'm starting a horse in a new movement, I am most concerned with the correct motion, no matter how ragged it is. As in side-passing, I start with motion to the left. Turning to the right seems to be harder for most horses, and because I want to build a horse's confidence, I start him to the left, the path of least resistance. Remember, for the moment I am only concerned with motion to the left. I can refine the actual footwork later. In the beginning I don't want to confuse my horse by demanding too much. That's why the horse is in the stall. Circling the edge of the stall gives him the idea of motion in a confined space. The walls hold the horse in the correct position, just as they did when he was learning to side-pass. Then I can stay off the horse's mouth and keep it soft and receptive.

We talk about correct motion and refining footwork, but what is actually the correct motion for a horse spinning? Ideally the horse moves quickly around his inside hind foot, which is his pivot foot. The front feet cross each other, and the free hind foot pushes the horse's body around *(photo 26)*. A dressage rider would call it a pirouette, the forehand moving around the inside hind leg. Now the pivot foot is turning and moving slightly, because the horse is moving his hind feet in a small circle while his front feet are moving in a larger circle. However, the hind feet should not move backward or sideways.

I have seen a very few horses clamp that pivot foot in the ground and spin correctly the first time. To teach this horse to spin correctly and use his rear end, to shift his weight onto his hindquarters, I bring the horse down to smaller and smaller circles and then tap him with a bat just behind my leg. (I use a light crop instead of spurs, because I don't use my feet for cuing. I use my legs and keep my feet at a balanced point to hold me in position over the horse's center of balance.) I let the horse move under me.

When a reining horse is really spinning, it is almost impossible to use your feet for anything but holding your position. The bat shouldn't bother the horse, but if he starts forward he'll still give his head to the reins and go half a turn. If he does go out of his circle like this, I take the horse back to the wall of the box stall for a few circuits and tap again. All the tapping does is increase the impulsion to the left. One tap on the horse's right side just behind my leg, and if he does a three-quarter turn, that's great.

I don't want to go to the bit or bosal to create this motion to the left. I don't want to haul the horse around. I want the impulsion to come from the rear; that's why I use the crop behind my leg. Each time a horse does a

three-quarter turn and stops, I back him a step or two. This also encourages him to keep his weight on his hindquarters and not fall onto his forehand. The whip also encourages the horse to move away from the pressure while staying on his hind feet.

Horses with a naturally low head carriage usually want to go on their forehand. I'll hold these horses a little tighter to give them some support in the front. If they still turn their hindquarters and wallow around on the forehand, I'll whack them on the front shoulder and then quickly behind the girth the moment I ask for a spin, and at the same time I'll pick up the head with a stronger contact. This should shift the weight off the horse's forehand and toward the rear.

Once the horse is turning around in the box stall, I'll start demanding more impulsion. I want him "looking for more," even if I must sacrifice some smoothness for this extra speed and power. I don't want him to go too fast, though. I ask for more impulsion to put an edge on him so he'll pick up his front feet and move around his hindquarters. With the extra impulsion, he'll find it easier to swing his body around. To increase the impulsion I use the crop once—hard—then I don't use it again until I really need it. After one fast spin, I go back to working slower and trying for more smoothness.

When the horse is getting the correct motion to the left in the box stall, I take him into the arena. As usual, I walk him in a very small circle so he can see and become familiar with his surroundings. This is preparation for what is to come next. When I ask for a spin I try to keep his head straight, but I don't expect him to be perfect. I ask him to turn two or three times, and then I take him back into the box stall. I ask him to spin there once at speed, and then I put him up. This leaves him with the ideas of motion and success on his mind. Because it is easier for him to hold his position in a stall, we have ended on a good note. I may do this for three or four days, and then when I take him outside to work I'll really see improvement.

Each time I spin him in the arena, I back the horse a few steps. This encourages him to stay back on his hindquarters with his hind legs under him. It is a way of making anticipation, usually a fault, work *for* me. I won't ask the horse to back after a spin in competition—I'll just hold him in place with my legs—but the anticipation of backing keeps him in balance. Only when you make a habit of spinning and then cantering right out of it each time does the horse begin to anticipate in a way that will harm him. If he thinks he will canter out of each spin, he will soon start moving out before the spin is finished. This causes him to fall onto his forehand. By encouraging him to anticipate a backward motion, I keep him in balance.

When the horse is turning lightly and easily outside the box stall—picking up his feet, holding his head and neck in a straight line, getting the motion—then I quit and begin working on a spin in the other direction. I do the spin to the right exactly the way I did the spin to the left. When I am working him to the right in the stall, I remind him of his spin to the left once before I put him up for the day. Because he can spin in this direction easily it builds confidence, and it also builds a connection in his mind between the two movements he is being asked to do.

People who aren't right-handed might have trouble teaching a horse to spin to the right. If this is the case with you, bridge the reins and give the horse more support with the outside rein. This direction might be a little more difficult for both horse and rider, but never lose your temper with the horse. No matter how he is carrying his head, never use the bat on his head or nose to correct head position. If you feel yourself losing control of your emotions, just get off, put the horse up, and quit for the day.

It is safe to ask a horse to spin every day, as long as you do it at different speeds and for a very short time. One day I work on basics: motion, coordination, form. The next day I'll ask for speed, and this is where you have to use some sense. When you ask a horse hard, the spin won't be as pretty *(photo 27),* but don't punish him for not being pretty. The horse is more excited; he is looking for more ground to cover.

This is where the hands come in. Your hands must be used to guide the horse in the correct motion and keep him in the area of the spin. If you are insecure in your seat and are using the reins for balance, you will be pulling your horse all over the arena without realizing it . . . until you stop and find yourself thirty feet from where you started. Beginning reining riders will swear up and down that they didn't *even touch* the reins during the spin, but the evidence is there when the horse travels during the spin.

The next day, after asking the horse for speed, soft-peddle him. A horse gives out quickly when he is being asked to spin. He loses wind quickly. When he has done it right, let him alone. Go out and trail-ride him. Do some Western Riding patterns or just pleasure-ride him in big circles. Most faults that horses commit at the spin come from exhaustion, and the exhaustion comes from being asked to spin and spin and spin by inconsiderate riders.

Another movement to teach the horse is the rollback. This is the Western equivalent of a demi-pirouette, a 180-degree turn on the hindquarters. The horse stops,

turns 180 degrees on his pivot foot, the front feet crossing each other, and then canters out of it on the opposite lead. (Performance classes often call for a pivot. This is essentially the same movement as a rollback—but performed slowly, usually at the walk.)

I find it easier to teach the horse to spin first and then release him early into a rollback than to teach the rollback and then try to drive the horse into a full spin. When the horse is spinning easily in both directions, I start my rollbacks. I teach my horse in whatever bit I have him in—a gag or a short-shanked snaffle. I don't work him in a bosal because I want more control over my stop, and a bosal just doesn't supply the precision I want.

To bring my horse into the correct position for a rollback, I put him into a canter on the left lead and circle him to the left. When he is relaxed and established in his gait, I say "Whoa," feel with my reins, and let him stop. I don't jerk him down, but I do use my legs to keep his hind legs under him. The instant he is stopped I ask him to turn to the right, and when I ask him to turn I'll smack him with the bat just behind my left leg. It isn't going to be a spin, but I want the same amount of impulsion I would get when spinning. I want the horse to lunge forward a little. As he spins three quarters of the way around, I'll push him with my left leg and ask for the right lead. Then I release him from his spin and canter him out on a straight line. If he doesn't pick up the correct lead, I just let him go and try to switch him over or even drop back into a trot and pick it up then.

When he has mastered this, I begin again on the reverse to the inside of the circle. I repeat it three or four times to give the horse the idea. This variation on the spin gives the horse more variety in his work, while still working on the same basic skill. Rollbacks can be used in conjunction with his work in the stall, and they will probably enhance his work there.

If you dissected it, a rollback would look like this: canter, stop, turn, and come out on the correct lead. If you turn to the left, come out on the left lead. If you turn to the right, come out on the right lead. Come out cantering, not running. Come out on a straight line, not on a curve. This is your basic starting rollback *(photos 28–31)*.

It takes about two months to master. Bring the horse out of his stall, warm him up, two-track and side-pass him, spin, and practice your rollback. At this point, when the spin and rollback have been mastered, you leave the work in the box stall forever. The only time you would take the horse back into the stall would be for a reminder if he hasn't been worked in a long time and has forgotten his cues.

Each day, the horse progresses or he doesn't progress. As a trainer, you just have to use your common sense and hold your temper. Both horse and rider will have good days and bad days. Teaching a horse to spin and roll back is a long and exhausting procedure. It takes a horse a month to go from walking around his stall to picking up his feet and staying back on his hindquarters. Most of the mistakes a horse makes come from being asked to spin when he is tired, and a horse gets tired quickly when spinning. After reviewing his earlier lessons, I work the horse in a stall or outside on a spin for an average of 10 minutes a day. One way at a time. One direction at a time. At least one month to the left. At least one month to the right.

28

29

10. SLIDING STOPS

Perhaps more than any other movement, the sliding stop is the mark of the Western reining horse. Gathering his hindquarters under him with increasing power and impulsion, the horse braces his hind legs and slides along the arena's surface, walking with his front legs and balancing his weight and the rider's. The slide must be straight and smooth with no stumbling or falling. The horse must receive the rider's cue for the stop without opening his mouth excessively, jawing, or raising his head. At the same time, the rider must give the cue easily without jerking the reins, putting both hands on the rein (except in hackamore classes), or holding onto the saddle.

The sliding stop is also the hardest to explain and the hardest to perform. If you have brought your horse this far as an amateur, you have done a terrific job, but unless you have a wealth of experience in showing reining horses in serious competition, or have apprenticed with a professional, you almost have to send your horse to a trainer to learn the sliding stop. For most people, I hope this chapter will be of academic interest only. It is possible to buy the kind of stop rig I use *(photo 32)*, and you can use the same kind of program in conjunction with a bosal or bit. But for most people even the mildest kind of

equipment can become the razor blade in the monkey's paw when they try to teach a sliding stop. I can only repeat that if you don't have a lot of experience and supervision, *teaching* the sliding stop to a prospective reining horse is something that almost invariably must be left to a professional who specializes in this kind of training.

A sliding stop depends on the rider's coordination and balance as well as that of the horse. Although it isn't performed at great speed, there is a lot of drive coming from the rear of the horse, a lot of power being generated and thrust forward. As rider, your seat must be completely secure, allowing the hands to be light, sensitive, and independent, because the whole feel of the stop is in your hand. You must know when to release the horse and when to pick him back up again and give him support through the reins. You must know when the horse needs help in balancing and when he must be left alone. And these decisions aren't made only once in a sliding stop. They are made and acted upon many times in the course of a twelve-foot slide.

Another factor to consider is facilities. You can be the most talented rider in the world, but without the right surface for the horse to work on, you can literally cripple the horse. If you try to make do and school the horse in an open field or in an arena with deep, heavy soil, forget it. In reining, you want the horse to slide along the top of the ground. It's prettier and it's easier on the horse's legs. If he is worked on a poor surface in the backyard riding ring, the horse is automatically put in a dangerous situation. You ask for a stop, the horse hesitates in the uncertain footing, you get mad and pull—you'll get the horse to stop, all right. The horse stops all at once, rips his back feet into the ground, and smashes his nose through the bridle. So for the horse's sake and your own sake, don't be satisfied with anything less than a perfect surface: hard-packed clay cushioned with several inches of sand or tanbark.

Before the horse is even ready for this surface, I do a lot of *preliminary* training for the stop. At this time the horse knows what "Whoa" means and will stop on command, but now I want to teach him to *prepare* for a stop. I want to be able to warn him that a stop is coming up so he can get his hind legs underneath him and brace for the slide.

I start this preparation in an arena that has good footing. The horse is bitted in a short-shanked snaffle with the usual rawhide mouthpiece. After warming up the horse, I start trotting him around the arena *(photo 33).* When I get him on the long straight side I say "Whoa" and take up a contact on his mouth. I don't jerk him, I just hold his head and squeeze with my legs to bring his hindquarters underneath him.

The minute the horse comes to a stop, I back him quickly. If he has a tendency to come onto his forehand, I take my feet out of the stirrups as we're trotting. I'll say "Whoa" as before, but as he stops I will reach out with both feet and tap him smartly on the shoulders *(photo 34).* Then I back him. This reinforces the idea that backing immediately has given him: to shift his weight onto his hindquarters when he stops.

I repeat this several times. I trot him around, say "Whoa," stop him, and back. Pretty soon all I have to do is say "Whoa" and I can feel the horse preparing, getting his feet under him and shifting his weight onto the

33

34

hindquarters. This takes a while, though. It takes a couple of weeks to make a horse's tendency to anticipate work for you and for him.

When I've reached the point where the horse is stopping easily from a trot and an extended trot, I can move up to a canter. I canter the horse down the long side of the arena or down the center line, say "Whoa," take up a contact on the reins, and push him backward. Between stops I ride a lot of circles at the trot and canter, which keeps this anticipation under control. But though I ride the horse in circles, I never try to stop a horse on a curve, because it throws him off-balance. Instead I ride several circles until I feel the horse relaxing, and then I take him off the circle onto a straight line before asking for the stop and back.

At about this point I introduce another signal to stop, another way to prepare the horse for the slide. When we're going down the straight side, I'll tap him with my leg: *One, two.* This will be the warning signal: *One, two,* "Whoa" + rein contact = stop. This leg signal gives the horse advance warning of the request to stop. I don't use it a lot, but it is a signal I want my horses to know.

Now I am ready to take my horse to a surface that will allow him to scoot along the ground and learn to balance himself. It took me a while to find this surface, and when I did it turned out to be on a racetrack ten miles from the stable. Each time I work a horse on sliding stops, I put the horse in the trailer and take him over there. I don't take a chance on working anywhere else, especially with my young horses. (This doesn't mean that any racetrack automatically makes the best surface for teaching the sliding stop. It's just a lucky coincidence that this one does.)

Before beginning my stopping at the racetrack, I have the farrier shoe the horse with plain shoes in front and sliding plates behind. The first plates I put on are three-quarter-inch with a rolled toe. The degree of angle on the hind foot, if I can get it, is 50 degrees on a young horse and 48 degrees on an older one. The front feet I leave at 50 degrees. (Some trainers jerk the shoes off the front feet, cut the hooves down to the blood, and let the horse ouch along. They believe this will encourage the horse to keep his weight on his hindquarters and lighten the forehand. Besides being despicable, this trick doesn't work. Making the forefeet so sensitive encourages the horse to snatch up his feet as soon as they make contact with the ground, or to prop. Another cause of propping—a serious fault in reining horses—is stopping the horse on a surface that won't allow him to slide.)

A three-quarter-inch plate is as much as a green reining horse can handle at this time in his training. I leave the inside of the hoof a little higher than the outside to help the horse hold a straight line and to prevent his feet from sliding apart. I also roll the toe slightly, but not into the hoof. As the horse braces himself to stop, the first thing that hits is the rolled toe, which sets the horse back on the sliding plate behind. (Ask the farrier to fill the roll with plastic wood for a neater hoof.) I don't turn up the shoes' edges behind, because most horses step on those trailers and pull the shoes off. When finishing horses shod with sliding plates, the farrier should rasp off the nailheads close to the hoof to keep them from catching. This means he'll have to use a bigger nail, but it's worth the trouble. Later, when the horse is more experienced, I'll go to a one-inch plate, but that's as big as I'll go.

When I finally begin the actual sliding stop, I want to be careful not to burn the back of the horse's ankles. One bad burn and it's unlikely that the horse will want to stop and slide again. To prevent this injury, I wrap the hind pasterns with cotton, just covering the ankle and into the pastern. Obviously, the reining horse isn't supposed to get down deep enough to injure himself—he should just slide along the top of the ground. But at first the horse might have trouble balancing himself and stumble, so I put skid boots over the bandages on the hind legs. I wrap the front legs over a brace of Listerine if the horse begins to show signs of soreness or stiffness there. If the horse has a tendency to strike himself or overreach, I use bell boots over the exercise bandages on the front legs.

At the other end of the horse, I am using a short-shanked snaffle bit with the rawhide mouthpiece. I don't like to use a bit with a solid port. When I turn a horse, I like the flexibility of a "broken" or jointed snaffle. I also like a swivel port. For the finished horse, I can use a straight bar bit with a swivel on the side, but a bar bit is a severe bit, and you have to know how to use it. If that bit is yanked it will cut the horse's tongue for sure. Your hands have to be light, and this is another reason for practicing on experienced horses before going to a bar bit (or any other bit on a young horse). A bit is not there to hold you in the saddle. It is a means of communication between you and the horse, and that line of communication must be used very tactfully.

In the beginning the horse is wearing a snaffle with a tie-down, which will help him hold himself in balance and keep his head down. Some people like to use a hacka-more bit at this stage, but I don't like them. It's easy to use them too strongly, and a hackamore bit can easily cut off a horse's air.

The first time or two I ask a horse to stop on a sliding surface, I use a stop rig, an "easy stop bit" *(see photo 32)*. This rig fits right under the chin with a rope over the horse's nose. It gives the horse something to brace against while protecting his mouth. The pressure is put on the chin groove instead of on the sensitive bars of the mouth. This is not to say that the easy stop isn't a potentially severe piece of equipment. It is. It can exert terrific leverage not only on the chin groove but also on the poll. In no way do I think this rig is appropriate for the inexperienced amateur, but it *is* what I use and find to be very successful in the right—and extremely light—hands.

When the horse arrives at the racetrack I use for teaching the sliding stop, I trot him around the area to get him used to the place. One thing a racetrack does is give you some scope to work your horse down. If a horse wants to run, some trainers *make* him run, then run a little faster than the horse wants to, until he is ready to slow down. A place like a racetrack "airs him out" and allows a horse to get all the running out of his system before you settle down to work.

A galloping warmup is only for the few days when the horse might be hot and excited. It is not by any means an everyday routine. If a horse is galloped every day he will come to expect it each time he is worked or competed, and this is going to cause a lot of problems. But in crisp weather or after his rest day, this particular track helps me accomplish two things: By the time my horse has finished being breezed for a while he is looking for a place to stop, and the surface helps him stop correctly.

When the horse is warmed up (or cooled off) I trot him

slowly down the track on a straight line. I give him the warning taps with my leg, say "Whoa," squeeze with my legs, and take up a contact of an inch or two on the reins, according to the lightness of the horse. Some horses need a firm hold, others a very light one. If this is your first time using a stop rig, you will be amazed at what a light touch it needs. Until both you and your horse become used to it, just touch the reins lightly, as if you were touching a red-hot burner on the stove. Work slowly. Just trot out, stop, and rest a few minutes.

When the horse is going fast enough—he should have enough speed at the extended trot—and with the plates on his hind feet, his hind legs will begin to slide under him when I call for the stop. As these legs, carrying a lot of the horse's body weight, slide toward the front feet, the horse will pick up the front feet to get them out of the way. (Just as when he is side-passing, he will move the right foot over as the left foot crosses over.)

After a few times, I can get rid of the stop rig I have been using with a tie-down. After three or four days at the trot, I'll need an even lighter contact with the reins to ask for a stop. I will just barely be feeling the horse's mouth. At this point I am using my hand solely as a balancing point. I am holding the horse's chin lightly, letting him "walk" in front and slide behind. I want to encourage this slide and help him maintain it for as far as possible. This is what we want in Western reining today, not that deep stop of the past with the horse's head up and his back often hollow.

When I move on to the canter, I'll go back to the easy stop for the first few tries. I'll ask the horse to canter slowly down the straightaway. I'll give him the warning signal, say "Whoa," and take up the rein contact very lightly. By now, even at a different gait, the horse knows what the signals mean and is preparing to stop. As he begins to slide, I squeeze with the calves of my legs and come a little forward in the saddle *(photo 35)*. Just as in jumping, the momentum is pushing me forward and I give to it. I'm forward just enough to let the horse's hindquarters work freely. I barely leave the saddle, but all my weight is on my legs and feet.

An important thing to keep in mind now is speed, or lack of it. Even when the horse is fully trained, I never run him full out. Even if he is a terrific stopper, this horse still has to be balanced, and the faster he's moving when I ask for the stop, the harder this balance is going to be to achieve. Excessive speed leads to a lot of problems in reining patterns in general and in sliding stops in particular. Too much speed is one reason so many people cannot stop their horses correctly. They ask their horses for too much speed and end up blowing past their stops because the horse is off-balance or is charging the stop.

Charging the stop comes from a combination of excessive speed and the practice of always stopping the horse in the same place or in the same sequence of movements. Because he is off-balance, stopping is an unpleasant experience, and the horse wants to get it over with quickly. Because he is always stopped in the same place (or at the same time) the horse knows where he has to go in order to get it over with quickly. Consequently, he races to the appointed place even faster, making a sliding stop even more difficult. And so the problem gets worse each time.

Excessive speed and a tactless rider lead to another common and serious fault in sliding stops: The horse opens his mouth and pokes his nose in the air. Both these

head resistances come from the tactless rider's *demanding* a stop, instead of asking and preparing his horse for one. Such a rider doesn't prepare the horse with the legs or a verbal command but relies only on hands and the power of the bit. This is like racing the horse into a brick wall, and it gets the same results.

It is tempting to run a horse flat out and stop, but I stop mine out of a trot for about a month. If the horse stops badly (and knows better) I back him quickly. Backing quickly is hard work, and doing more work is his punishment—just as resting and not having to work for a few minutes is the horse's reward. I don't beat my horse in the mouth. I don't slap him on the side of the head. I just ask him to back a little faster and a little farther than usual.

Spending a month stopping from a trot and slowly working up to a canter takes time, but it is a safe method. Just as in spinning, I keep building the horse's muscles, confidence, and reactions until the movement is smooth, strong, and balanced.

11. COMPETITION REINING

There are very few riders who buy or train reining horses just to ride around the backyard. Just as with those who work with racehorses or gymkhana horses or three-day event horses, people who are serious about reining devote much of their effort to competition and to preparing for it. This doesn't mean that a trainer's talents at training and riding are necessarily going to be equal, at any level. There are quite a few professional riders who have a hard time training, and there are lots of good amateur trainers who go to pieces at the thought of showing.

The biggest problem for you as an amateur rider/trainer is nerves, and the panic often begins as soon as the horse seems ready to compete. It isn't easy to decide whether to take a horse into a Reining class, and it needs a lot of consideration. I don't enter a class unless I am sure the horse can do every movement in the pattern and do it well. For the first time out, I choose small, breed-approved shows. Even with green horses, I am building for the Nationals and the world competition. I want to get the feel of my green horses in competition, and I want them to get a lot of good ring experience. The horse needs to find out how he will be signaled in a show arena, and I need to know how he is going to respond there. A show like the New York Breeders in Syracuse is excellent for this, because the arena surface is good for reining. At a place like that I know the horse will have a lot of good facilities going for him.

Too often, the amateur takes a green horse to a small local show and jerks the horse's head off on ground he can't handle. Backyard shows are fine for getting experience in Western Riding or Pleasure, but they rarely have the surface needed for safe reining. So for the long run as well as the short run, spend the extra money and go to the name shows with the prepared arenas.

Another common stumbling block is an excess of enthusiasm. Just before the show the competitor decides that if a three-quarter-inch sliding plate shoe is good, more will make the stop *really* pretty. But the horse is not prepared for the extra slide the shoe will give him, and he is not strong enough or experienced enough to handle it yet. When he starts to slide, his shoes are so slick he can't control his hind legs and hold them straight. He starts to come out of the ground, his legs start to spread, and he lurches onto his forehand to keep himself from falling.

The bit is another thing that shouldn't be changed at the last minute. Almost every horse is going to be more excited at a show than he is at home, and almost every rider toys with the idea of going to a stronger bit just for the show. But with this stronger bit, the rider may forget to make allowances for it, ram the horse in the ground, and scare the daylights out of him. Or the rider can compound the problem by pulling up instead of back on the reins, lifting the horse's nose up and out of balance. If the rider ahead of me goes in and makes a spectacular run, something I know my horse can't beat, I don't try changing tack at the last minute in hopes of finding the magic bit. I don't ask the horse to stop any harder than he can stop. I only do what the horse can do. If I have to settle for second place, so be it. I can be happy with that, and besides, there will always be a next time.

What I do take a long look at before competition is the horse himself. I'm different from most reining-horse trainers. I like a nice, long tail and I like the mane pulled and the socks clipped. I want my horse to be good-looking, especially when he goes into competition. I think a good appearance helps in the arena. If a pretty horse can really do it, that horse is going to get scored higher than the average-looking horse that can really do it.

Some trainers and other competitors like to see how scroungy they can get their horses to look with long, long manes and ragged tails. They never seem to brush their horses. What they don't realize is that the horse's skin is an organ, just like the heart and lungs. By keeping him clean, I'm keeping him healthy as well as pretty. If I expect a horse to give his best, I have to pay attention to his skin as well as to his feed and shoeing.

Look at it another way. I think that if a horse is going to reward me with a good go, I should reward him by keeping him clean. It's a way of showing my appreciation I think a horse works better if he's clean. I like to be clean, I like to look nice, and a horse is no different. If a horse feels nice, he can work nice, and whether you know it or not, a horse likes to look nice. He may not say so, but I think he does.

As for myself, I don't want to detract from my horse or his performance by looking like I've just come in from doing the stalls. If I'm riding a good horse that is going to get the job done, I want to look nice. I wear good chaps, a nice hat, and a flashy shirt. I used to go into the ring wearing old, ragged chaps, but now I try to keep myself looking presentable because I'm representing a client and a client's good horse. If I look clean and neat, it will enhance the horse and make a better picture.

When I go to the Nationals, or to any show, I am aware of my horse's weaknesses. I know if he is a little weak on his spin and just how far he can slide. I know his lead changes will be good. (If I can't take lead changes for granted, I don't show the horse until I can.)

The first day of the show, I just ride the horse easily, keeping the edge off him by doing his usual warm-up routine and riding him in big circles. I let the horse look at everything and take his time getting used to the surroundings. I take him into the arena and let him look around and be spooky if he wants to. This relaxed work goes on for one or two days, if possible.

The day before his Reining class, I work him hard, sharpening up his spins and stops. I often go back to the trot for his stop work. I trot, stop, back, sit a minute, then spin. I work on these basics hard: the trot, slide, and rollback. I do lots of circles and maybe even a sliding stop from the canter. The only thing I don't practice is the actual pattern itself. It is just like preparing for a dressage test: Practice each movement but don't go over and over the test itself. Once is enough for a practice run-through if you think you need it.

At this point, don't try to teach the horse something new or try a completely new way of doing a movement, no matter what you see anybody else doing. If he has been prepared correctly, he is ready to do anything you ask. If he hasn't been prepared correctly, it's too late to do anything about it as far as this show is concerned.

The morning before the class, I take the horse out and just ride circles and relax him in a nice, enjoyable ride. Then I put him away. An hour before the class I get the horse out of his stall, brush him, and clean out his feet. I walk and trot him around, and then I spin him hard both ways two or three times. I find a good place and stop him. And right after that I put somebody else on him to walk him around and keep him relaxed. Because of this, my horse goes into the arena fresh, but not too fresh. He is responsive and will usually do the best he can.

Too many people wear their horses out in the warm-up arena. When they get to a horse show, they lose all their common sense, and the usual way they lose it is to leave all their reining pattern work outside the arena. These riders get too nervous and work their horses too hard. Some of these kids go nuts spinning their horses, maybe trying to scare the competition or maybe because in their excitement they want a little more from their horse than is there.

I turn my horse twice, stop him, and then forget him. I give him to somebody else. That's where I have an advantage: I have somebody to help me. I stay off my horse because, like everybody else, I have a tendency to pick at any horse I'm on before going into a class. I get on my horse, I tune him up, and then I stay away from him until we go into the class.

I don't mind going in first—doing the first pattern of the class and putting pressure on people. But a lot of amateurs get upset if they have to go before or after Roger Johnson or someone else who is well-known. They'll work themselves and their horses into a state of exhaustion because of this.

If I have to follow someone I know is pretty good, I go

where I can't watch him. I stick my fingers in my ears so I can't hear the crowd. I want to go into that arena stone cold, not knowing what the previous scores are. I want to ride my pattern according to my strategy without any pressure. If I'm in the finals, I know I'll have to ask a lot of my horse. I'll have to ask him for all he can give, but that's all. I don't want to be tempted to ask for more.

At the Appaloosa Nationals there are twelve finalists in reining. If I make the finals and I'm scheduled eighth or tenth, I might watch the first horse go, just to get an idea of how they're scoring. But if I'm second I don't watch. I get out of the arena. I don't want to be tempted to ride for the judge instead of riding for the horse. All I can really get out of a horse is what I've put into him and what he has himself. A trained horse won't usually try to mess up his rider. Most of the mistakes made in the arena are the rider's fault.

Under pressure, lots of riders seem to lose their common sense. If the reining pattern calls for a run in and stand twenty feet off the wall, why do they persist in running right down the wall as close as they can get to it? I can tell my students not to ride for the wall, and still they are drawn to it like a magnet. If you have this problem, compensate for it. Make a conscious effort to keep twenty feet from the wall, if that is what is required.

One way to do this is to put the horse on the correct lead. Most people walk in and don't care which lead they take if they canter on a straight line. Instead, start this canter on the lead away from the wall, and it will help keep the horse from hugging the wall.

If the pattern calls for a stop and back, don't run backward at 500 miles an hour. And don't back any farther than the pattern requires. Any judge will penalize heavily the rider who runs backward an extra fifty feet just to show off. Don't lose your head. Back quietly and concentrate on the job at hand. Just as in dressage, accuracy plays a big part in determining your reining score. If you are required to stop at X, X is where you stop. You don't get extra points for stopping at C instead.

As I settle the horse, I take a second look at the arena's surface. I want to find a clear path to the sliding stop. Nine times out of ten, when several horses have gone ahead they've made a hole in the dirt where they stopped. Amateurs tend to ignore this hazard and run straight for that hole. They don't bother to find new ground to stop on. Naturally, the horse won't be able to slide when he hits that hole, and he will lose points on that movement. It's just like riding a hunter on an outside course. If six other horses have dug a hole at a jump's takeoff point, move your horse over a little so he avoids hitting it and slipping.

Another factor in accuracy is the pylon. Pylons are used to help the rider, just like the letters in a dressage arena. But to many riders they are a hazard. I go deep beyond the pylon so that when I do the rollback around it I have plenty of clearance. A lot of people, however, run *at* a pylon instead of *to* it, just like with the wall. They stop their horse, do a rollback, and barely miss hitting the marker. More often than not they knock it over and get disqualified.

This is a natural mistake for an inexperienced rider of reining horses, but there is no excuse for missing a lead. Admittedly, both horse and rider are going to be on edge and thinking about the crowd and the judge. But no matter how much tension there is, take time to side-pass a step, to take up a contact on the reins and make that horse listen a little before he takes his lead in the first figure eight. Before I ask for a canter, I get control of the horse's head and sides. It takes a second or two, but when I start out I don't already have points against me for an incorrect lead.

Keep the horse upright for a lead change and go for smoothness instead of speed. It's too easy to let the crowd affect you. Beginning riders are often frozen by the crowd. They kick the horse off into a canter as unconcerned about leads as they can be. When they miss that first lead, they ride harder and faster trying to make up for it, instead of correcting it or getting it right next time. Some people get into trouble with lead changes because they don't keep the horse upright. They just dig in the spur and throw him over, hoping to get onto the right lead but usually just getting off-balance.

The last part of a reining pattern is presenting the bit to the judge for inspection. This is to prevent an illegal bit or curb chain from winning the class. Some riders drop the bit and then just sling the bridle under the horse's neck and trot out of the ring like that. It looks pretty dashing, but even if I'm in a hurry I like to put the bit back in my horse's mouth. I like to leave the arena with the bit on because I don't want to take a chance on the horse getting away from me. Even after a good reining pattern, it's pretty embarrassing to have to chase your horse down when he has taken off around the arena with the bridle hanging around his neck.

But no matter what happens, one thing I pride myself on is that I don't whip or jerk my horse during the class if he doesn't do exactly what I want him to. Sure, I might get irritated, but the show ring is not the place to discipline an animal. The mistake has been made, and all the whipping in the world won't erase it. I just hand the horse to someone else and get away from him. Fifteen minutes later, most people will realize that a large part of it was probably the rider's mistake. Put the horse up. Take him home. Train him better. The only thing losing your temper at a horse show proves is what a fool you are.

The final aspect of successful showing is souring and how to avoid it. One of the hardest things to get a feel for is how much work is enough. That's one of the benefits of working with a trainer. The professional can quickly spot the signs of early boredom in a reining horse and keep you from contributing to the biggest cause of souring: overuse of the horse at home.

For instance, once the horse has learned to stop correctly, don't practice it a lot. Don't rein or spin your horse into the ground. This is the biggest advantage of emphasizing versatility among Western breeds. Versatility encourages riders to enter many different events instead of overspecializing. I don't have too much trouble with souring, because I compete my reining horses in similar events like Western Riding and Western Pleasure. The thing to keep in mind once you have produced a good Western reining horse is that he can stay on top for about three years. Compete him carefully and work him carefully. One good practice session is worth ten mediocre ones, and one big win is better than fifty little ones.

12. A REINING PATTERN— STEP BY STEP

I know my pattern. I've looked at the arena, and I know the best place to stop. I gather my horse outside the arena. The run in must be at least twenty feet from the arena wall, and I want to run a little beyond the center of the two pylons. That will give me ten or twelve feet to back up. . . .

They call my number. My name. The name of the horse.

I squeeze my horse off on the left lead. If he is on the right lead he'll drift toward the wall, so I want to make sure of that left lead on a pleasure-horse canter. I squeeze him once and begin releasing pressure on the reins. He's building speed now. I'm looking down the arena and planning where I'm going to stop. My horse is running but he is balanced on the bridle. Get ready. Warn him, *One, two, "Whoa," pull, stop.*

Okay, I'm past my center point and I've stopped my horse. I let him get all the way stopped and collected. Now I'm backing him and thinking, *Keep your legs on his sides.* I'm holding the horse in a tunnel formed by my reins and legs. If he backs a little crooked, I've got my legs right there to correct him. My horses give to the bridle, so I'm not worried about his throwing up his head and resisting. I'm backing this horse straight, using my legs and looking for the center of the pattern.

At the center I stop and release the reins on the horse's neck. He knows this means halt from his previous training. He halts and settles. He is standing still. He is relaxed but at the same time alert and ready to do something.

I settle my horse the full ten seconds allowed and then turn him to go directly to the middle of the arena. Don't shake him up here. Turn him nice and easy. Don't do a spin or a quarter-pivot turn, because it isn't called for in the pattern. I release my reins a little and, letting him walk forward a little, angle him off toward the center of the pattern.

I must start him off on the right lead, but my body is angled to the left. I don't want to make a mistake here, so I take hold of my horse's mouth and get him on the bit, in the bridle. I put my left leg on him and lift him into the right lead. I ease him off into the first loop of his first figure eight. This eight is smaller and slower than the second one, and I want the difference to be marked. I canter my horse collected, never wide open, so my first circle will be quite slow, almost a pleasure-horse canter. My second figure eight will be extended a little more.

Though this first circle is small, it isn't so small that it binds my horse and asks too much of him. I make sure the horse has space to canter and come up on a straight line for the lead change. I take my left rein and hold it against my horse's neck, holding his forehand in the original bend. (At this point, a reining-horse rider should be more concerned with positioning the horse for the smoothest transition, not with leads. Leads should be taken for granted.)

I come back around after the second loop and, on a straight line, ask for the lead change. I don't speed up or ask for an extended stride *before* the change. I hold the horse upright, change, *and then* urge the horse on to a bigger, faster figure eight, extending the circles up to the pylons. I don't come so close that the pylons are knocked over, though.

Coming in for my final loop, I tap the horse with my left foot so he won't anticipate the change and cut into it. I nudge him to get him upright. I don't want him anticipating the change and cutting the circle short. At this point a lot of people would take the change anywhere they could get it and run for the pylon. But I have to pay attention to detail and accuracy if I want to get a good score, so I am careful to close that last figure eight.

Only when I get the lead change do I go to the pylon. (If I go for the pylon before catching the hind lead as well as the front, I should be penalized heavily, but a lot of people making their transition from spectator to contestant don't realize this.) I run on to the pylon, all the time thinking to myself, *Go on beyond the pylon, Terry. Push the horse on. Don't ask for a stop too soon or you will run into the pylon when you turn.* Only when I am *at* the pylon do I even give the horse the warning, the *preparation* for the stop. Then I ask for the stop and slide him as far as I can (*photo 36*).

As he nears the end of his slide, I can feel the horse gathering himself up, getting his balance. Then I ask him to turn. I put the rein against his neck to turn him, and at the same time I touch him with my right foot just a little, to nudge him on around. As he turns, I release him and push him straight forward past the pylon, without hitting it.

I'm going down the arena, moving my horse so I can pass the other pylon. I am almost two-tracking my horse across the arena at the canter, more precisely leg-yielding at the canter, so I can come up on the correct side of the pylon. I tell myself, *Don't stop here, go on. Get to the pylon. Now stop the horse.* One, two, and let him slide all the way out.

If I don't catch the horse right to cue him for the stop, if he buckles and bounces, I just concentrate on getting him stopped as safely and as balanced as possible. I gather him up. I put this mistake out of my mind. I can make up my errors on my next stop. I get the horse stopped; then I nudge him with my left foot to turn him around and push him out of his rollback.

We're almost done, and I'm tempted to think, *Really run this horse and jerk him in the ground. Get all the points you can. Go for broke. Take a chance.* But then I say to myself, *No, Terry. Gather this horse up and get him moving freely with his hind legs moving under him. Not so fast that he can't balance himself properly, though, because you don't want to mess up your pattern here. You've had a nice go. Don't mess it up by asking too much of your horse.*

Almost as I am thinking this, I'm looking for that place where I can stop—not the place where five other horses have stopped and dug a trench in the arena, but a clean, level spot where my horse can slide. I see it. Nudge the horse: *One, two, "Whoa," stop.* When I stop him here and he has come to a halt, I drop my rein hand on his neck and release him.

I settle him for two seconds just so he can gather his mind together.

Here the pattern calls for a pivot. The pattern just says

PIVOT. Often beginners want to get the horse stopped and then do a little more than the pattern calls for, want to pivot right over themselves—*wham, wham.* They pull the horse onto his back legs too fast and mess up the pivot in their eagerness. It's smoother to let the horse move forward toward the judges a little to gather himself. Take hold of his mouth lightly to shift his weight evenly and get his balance. I'm going to make this pretty. I'm not going to ask or push too hard. I want my horse to walk around his hindquarters, foot over foot.

Now the pattern calls for a quarter turn. Pause here for just an instant. It's not noticeable, but that slight hesitation lets my horse gather his wits and coordination. Go too fast and the pivot will be sloppy and unbalanced.

I pivot in the other direction.

Then I release my horse and let him push off toward the judges. Trot him easy, just let him float forward. I drop my bridle for the judges to inspect the bit. I put the bridle back on.

And go on out of the arena.

THE APPALOOSA
HORSE CLUB PATTERNS

Although breed associations, horse show associations, and 4H occasionally differ slightly in their judging criteria for Western Riding and Reining, most of them are remarkably similar. With the kind permission of The Appaloosa Horse Club, here are some samples of riding and reining patterns and of what the judge looks for when judging these classes in most horse shows today.

WESTERN RIDING CLASS

To be judged: On the basis of 60 to 80 points, with 70 denoting an average score.

General Information

This class is a combination class which is designed to show characteristics of control and skills used in Equitation, Reining, and Trail classes. Further, it combines the maneuvers needed for a handy working ranch horse and rider.

Class Conditions and Rules

The class will enter the ring and line up at one end for the judge's inspection and directions. Following this the class will leave the ring. Each rider will re-enter the ring to perform the prescribed pattern individually. Each horse shall rein and handle easily, fluently, effortlessly, and with reasonable speed throughout the pattern.

Considerations for Judging

1. Change of leads (preference shall be given to flying changes of leads midway between the markers throughout the entire class.)

2. Smoothness of performance.

3. Steadiness of gaits and response to rider.

4. Knocking down of markers or obstacles will not disqualify a contestant but shall be scored accordingly by the judge.

5. Abusive use of the mouth of the horse shall be scored accordingly.

The use of the gate shall be optional with the local show committee according to local conditions.

On the pattern the short double line represents a swinging gate which the animal, on entering the arena, must put the rider in a position to open, pass through, and close without dismounting. The gate may be located in any convenient part of the arena where it will not interfere with the balance of the routine. Care should be exercised in selecting a gate which will not endanger horse or rider. The eight small circles represent markers (barrels, kegs, or standards recommended). These should be separated by a uniform distance of not less than thirty or more than fifty feet. The distance may be altered if local arena conditions are too small for the above distances. The rectangle represents an obstacle (one small log recommended) just high enough to break the animal's stride in going over. The long and sometimes twisting line

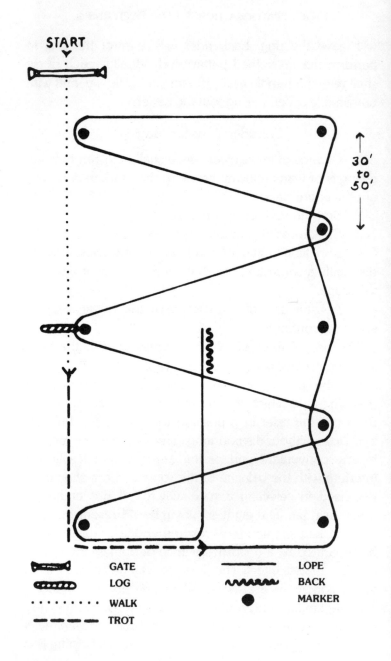

WESTERN RIDING CLASS PATTERN

indicates the direction to travel and the gaits at which the animal must move. The dotted line (. . .) indicates the walk, the dashed line (_ _ _) the trot, and the solid line (___) the lope. On entering the arena the exhibitor will put the animal through the gate and then proceed on the routine as indicated by the pattern. On completion he or she will ride to the judge as indicated by the judge. The judge may require an exhibitor to repeat or reverse any part of the routine. This is a judged event, not a timed event.

Note: It is permissible to change hands when opening a gate.

JUNIOR REINING CLASS

To be judged: On the basis of 60 to 80, with 70 denoting an average score.

General Information

Open to horses four years of age and under. Horses may be shown in either bit or hackamore at the discretion of the exhibitor. The judge shall have the authority to request any reining pattern which, in his or her opinion, better tests the reining ability of the horses entered. However, if additional reining patterns are used, it shall be so stated in the premium list that patterns other than the required reining patterns may be used.

Class Conditions and Rules

Horses are to be worked individually on the required Appaloosa Reining Pattern A, B, C, D, E, F, G, or H as illustrated. The judge may determine which reining pattern will be used. Each horse shall rein and handle easily,

fluently, effortlessly, and with reasonable speed throughout the pattern.

Note: Abusive use of the mouth of a reining horse
shall be scored accordingly.

Faults Against the Horse

1. Opening mouth excessively (when wearing bit).
2. Breaking gaits.
3. Refusing to change leads.
4. Anticipating signals.
5. Stumbling.
6. Switching tail.
7. Bouncing or sideways stop.
8. Backing sideways.
9. Nervous throwing of head.
10. Excessive jawing.
11. Halting or hesitating while being shown.
12. Knocking over stakes or keg markers.

Faults Against the Rider

1. Changing hands on reins.
2. Losing stirrup.
3. Two hands on reins at any time.
4. Any unnecessary aid given by the rider to the horse
(such as unnecessary talking, petting, spurring, quirting
with reins or romal, jerking of reins, etc.) to induce the
horse to perform will be considered a fault and scored
accordingly.
5. Touching horse or saddle with rider's hands while
horse is in motion.

Fall

A fall of horse and/or rider will result in disqualification.

SENIOR REINING CLASS

To be judged: On the basis of 60 to 80 points, with 70 denoting an average score.

General Information

Open to horses five years of age and older. All horses will be shown with a bit. The judge shall have the authority to request any reining pattern which, in his or her opinion, better tests the reining ability of the horses entered. However, if additional reining patterns are used, it shall be so stated in the premium list that patterns other than the required reining patterns may be used.

Class Conditions and Rules

Horses to be worked individually on the required Appaloosa Reining Pattern A, B, C, D, E, F, G, or H as illustrated. The judge may determine which reining pattern will be used. Each horse shall rein and handle easily, fluently, effortlessly, and with reasonable speed throughout the pattern. Any horse not following the exact pattern will be disqualified. Only one hand may be used on the reins and hands must not be changed. Hand to be around reins. One finger between reins permitted.

Note: Abusive use of the mouth of a reining horse shall be scored accordingly.

Faults Against the Horse

1. Opening mouth excessively in bit reining.
2. Breaking gaits.
3. Refusing to change leads.
4. Anticipating signals.
5. Stumbling.

6. Switching tail.
7. Bouncing or sideways stop.
8. Backing sideways.
9. Nervous throwing of head.

Faults Against the Rider

1. Changing hands on reins.
2. Losing stirrup.
3. Two hands on reins at any time.
4. Any unnecessary aid given by the rider to the horse (such as unnecessary talking, petting, spurring, quirting with reins or romal, jerking of reins, etc.) to induce the horse to perform will be considered a fault and scored accordingly.
5. Touching horse or saddle with rider's hands while horse is in motion.

Fall

A fall of horse and/or rider will result in disqualification.

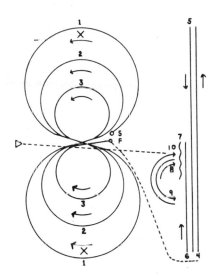

APPALOOSA REINING PATTERN A

Ride pattern as follows:

1. Large figure eight—with speed.
2. Small figure eight—with speed.
3. Still smaller figure eight—with speed.
4. Full run and sliding stop.
5. Full run and sliding stop.
6. Half run and sliding stop.
7. Back in tracks.
8. Pivot quarter turn to right.
9. Pivot half turn to left.
10. Pivot half turn to right; ride to judge for inspection.

X: Markers in middle of arena.

S: Start of figure eights.

F: Finish of figure eights.

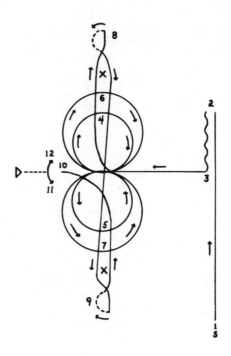

APPALOOSA REINING PATTERN B

Ride pattern as follows:

1. Run at full speed.
2. Stop and back.
3. Settle horse for 10 seconds.
4. and 5. Ride small figure eight at slow lope.
6. and 7. Ride large figure eight fast.
8. Left rollback over hocks.
9. Right rollback over hocks.
10. Stop.
11. Pivot left.
12. Pivot right; ride to judge for inspection.

X: Markers middle of arena.

S: Start.

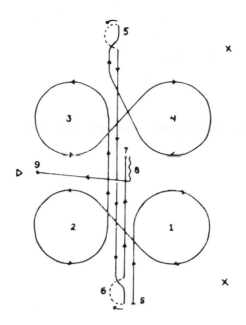

APPALOOSA REINING PATTERN C

Ride pattern as follows:

1. Ride circle to right, with speed, in correct lead.
2. Ride circle to left, with speed, in correct lead.
3. Ride circle to left, with speed, in correct lead.
4. Ride circle to right, with speed, in correct lead.
5. Left rollback over hocks.
6. Right rollback over hocks.
7. Run with speed; sliding stop.
8. Back and settle horse; ride to judge for inspection.
9. Ride to judge for inspection.

X: Rollback markers on arena wall.

S: Start.

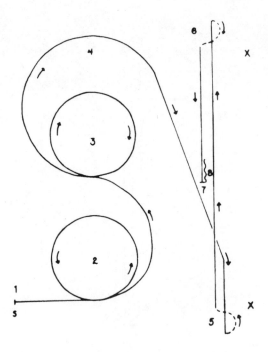

APPALOOSA REINING PATTERN D

Ride pattern as follows:

1. Start at lope.
2. Ride circle to left—slow.
3. Ride circle to right with speed.
4. Ride circle in correct lead with control.
5. Left rollback (stay at least 20 feet from arena wall).
6. Right rollback (stay at least 20 feet from arena wall).
7. Sliding stop; settle horse.
8. Back; ride to judge for inspection.

X: Rollback markers on arena wall.

S: Start.

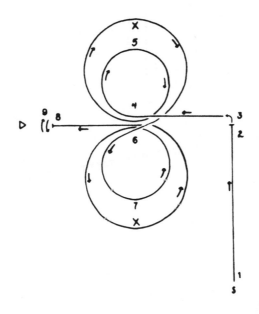

APPALOOSA REINING PATTERN E

Ride pattern as follows:

1. Run with speed.
2. Sliding stop; settle horse.
3. Quarter turn to left.
4. Ride small circle to right —slow.
5. Ride large circle to right with speed.
6. Ride small circle to left—slow.
7. Ride large circle to left with speed.
8. Sliding stop; settle horse.
9. Pivot left—pivot right; ride to judge for inspection.

X: Markers in middle of arena.

S: Start.

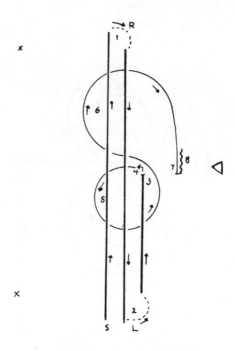

APPALOOSA REINING PATTERN F

Ride pattern as follows:

Run with speed.
1. Stop—pivot to right and run with speed.
2. Stop—pivot to left and run with speed.
3. Sliding stop.
4. Quarter-turn to left.
5. Begin slow circle to the left in correct lead.
6. Ride circle to right with speed in correct lead.
7. Sliding stop; settle horse.
8. Back; ride to judge for inspection.
X: Pivot markers on arena wall.
S: Start.

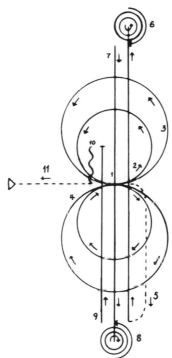

APPALOOSA REINING PATTERN G

Ride pattern as follows:

1. Walk to the center of the arena.
2. Starting to the right, ride a small figure eight at slow speed.
3. Ride second figure eight, larger and at faster speed.
4. At completion of second figure eight, pull up and go to the end of the arena to the judge's right.
5. Run with speed to opposite end of arena, with a straight stop past the end marker.
6. Do two complete spins to the left, then 180° pivot back to the right.
7. Run with speed to the opposite end of arena, with a straight stop past the end marker.
8. Do two complete spins to the right, then 180° pivot back to the left.
9. Run past marker in center of arena, with a straight stop.
10. Back 10 to 15 feet in straight line.
11. Ride to judge for inspection; dismount and drop bit from horse's mouth. Retire from arena.

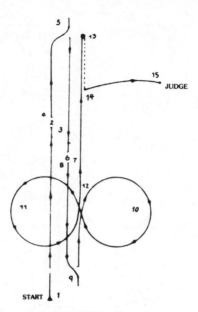

APPALOOSA REINING PATTERN H

•Mandatory marker on arena wall or fence.

The arena or plot should be approximately 50 by 100 feet in size. The judge shall indicate with markers on arena fence or wall the length of the pattern, but kegs or other markers within the area of the pattern will not be used.

Ride pattern as follows:

1. Run at full speed (should be run at least 20 feet from any fence or wall).
2. Stop.
3. Do a 360° spin.
4. Hesitate.
5. Proceed to the area beyond the point indicated by the marker on the arena wall or fence and do a left rollback over the hocks.
6. Stop.
7. Do a 360° spin.
8. Hesitate.
9. Proceed to the area beyond the point indicated by the other marker on the arena wall or fence and do a right rollback over the hocks.
10. and 11. Ride a figure eight.
12. and 13. Run at full speed.
13. Stop.
13. to 14. Back.
14. to 15. Walk to the judge and stop for inspection until dismissed.

150